DISCARD

Who?

Famous experiments
for the young scientist

Who?

Famous experiments for the young scientist

Robert W. Wood
Illustrated by Steve Hoeft

Chelsea House Publishers

Philadelphia

Library of Congress Cataloging-in-Publication Data

Wood, Robert W., 1933-
    Who? : experiments for the young scientist / Robert W. Wood :
illustrated by Steve Hoeft.
        p. cm.
    Originally published: Blue Ridge Summit. PA : TAB Books, 1995.
    Includes index.
    ISBN 0-7910-4851-9 (hardcover)
    1. Scientists—Experiments—History—Juvenile literature.
2. Engineering—Experiments—History—Juvenile literature.
3. Inventions—History—Juvenile literature. 4. Discoveries in
science—History—Juvenile literature. 5. Science—Exhibitions-
-Juvenile literature. I. Hoeft, Steve. II. Title.
Q164.W69 1997
306.43'0973

Contents

THE YOUNG CHEMIST

THE YOUNG PHYSICIST

Introduction

Science is a subject that instantly becomes exciting with even simple discoveries. We'll never know who discovered fire or invented the wheel. Discoveries sometimes happen by accident but most often are by design. The foundation of today's sciences came about through the efforts of experimenters in the past, beginning mostly in Europe in the sixteenth and seventeenth century. In earlier times, advances were often made by trial and error. But today, through education, we can avoid their failures and build on the accomplishments of people such as Galileo, Isaac Newton, Michael Faraday, and Marie Curie to name just a few. These scientists are not just names in a book, but real people who made exciting discoveries that make our comfortable lifestyle possible and provide building blocks for the future.

This book is part of a series of books that ask questions about science such as Why?, What?, When?, and Where? It provides experiments that relate to a few of the better known, and some lesser known, people that contributed to our scientific knowledge. It is divided into four parts, with each part relating to a different science. You should know, however, that any science will overlap to another. For example, an engineer needs to know something about physics, as well as a chemist. Each part of the book consists of easy experiments that begin by asking a question, followed by the materials list, a step-by-step procedure, and the results. At the end of each experiment you will find suggestions for further studies that will broaden the scope of the experiment, followed by science trivia for your amusement.

Symbols
used in this book

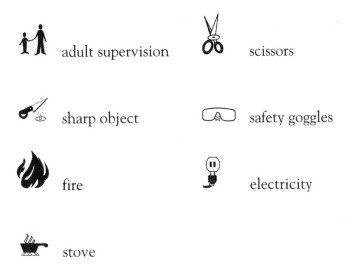

adult supervision

scissors

sharp object

safety goggles

fire

electricity

stove

Part 1
The young engineer

Egyptian builders began constructing the pyramids around 2,500 B.C. Around 200 B.C., Chinese military engineers used their skill to build the 1,400-mile- (2,260-km-) long, 20-foot- (6.1-m-) high fortification known as the Great Wall of China. Between 72 and 82 A.D., the Romans constructed their largest amphitheater, the Colosseum in Rome. This massive four-story arena could seat about 50,000 spectators. One of

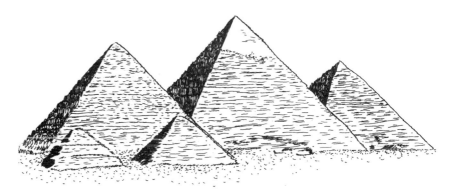

Ancient Egyptians built pyramids for the pharaohs and their closest relatives. These three are the tombs of Kings Menkaure, Khafre, and Khufu at Giza, near Cairo. The pyramid of Khufu, on the far right, is the largest in the world and was originally 482 feet (147 meters) high with each base measuring 756 feet (230 meters) long.

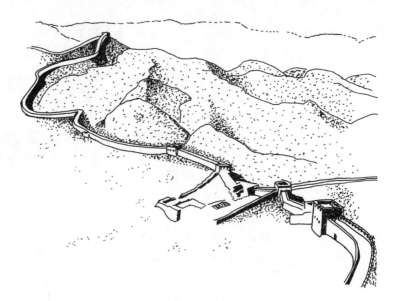

The Great Wall of China winds along the Mongolian plateau in western China to the Yellow Sea in the east. Beacons placed on watchtowers were used to summon soldiers to fight off invaders; however, the Ming dynasties ended when the Manchu were let through a gate by a traitor.

The Colosseum in Rome received its name because it was built next to a colossal 120-foot- (37.2-m-) high statue of Nero. The statue was later demolished. The Colosseum was 620 feet (189 m) long, 510 feet (156 m) wide, and 160 feet (49 m) high. It even had counterbalanced elevators for moving wild animals from chambers below the floor of the arena.

The Taj Mahal is built on a platform of about 313 square feet (29 sq. m) and rises to a height of 187 feet (57 m). It was built by Shah Jahan to serve as a mausoleum for his beloved wife Arjunand Banu Begum. She was known as Taj Mahal ("crown of the palace").

the most glorious buildings in the world, the Taj Mahal in Agra, India, was completed in 1648. Other engineering feats include the San Francisco–Oakland Bay Bridge and the Eiffel Tower in Paris. On a smaller but no less important scale, the Eskimos built igloos, the Sioux constructed tepees, the Apaches constructed wickiups, and the Indians of the Upper Great Lakes built wigwams.

Like these early pioneers, today's engineers are builders. They use their knowledge of science and art to put power and materials to work for the

The Eiffel Tower was built by French structural engineer Alexandre Gustave Eiffel for the Paris Exposition of 1889. The 984-foot (300-m) iron tower was designed so that bending and shearing forces of the wind were changed into forces of compression that the frame could better withstand.

benefit of society. Everyday things we take for granted—cars, airplanes, buildings—are the result of the design of engineers. They designed the projects, selected the materials, and determined that, whatever it was, it would stand up under the designated use.

Engineering includes many different fields, and several engineers may work on a single project. Mechanical engineers work with the design of machines, the strength of materials, and the use

Lillian Moller Gilbreth graduated from the University of California in 1900. She achieved many engineering "firsts" for women, including an honorary master of engineering degree from the University of Michigan and an honorary doctorate of engineering from Rutgers University. She was appointed the first woman delegate to the World Engineering Congress in Tokyo.

of gears and levers to accomplish work. Aeronautical engineers design the shape and structure of aircraft, while electronic engineers work with the instruments and guidance systems of the aircraft.

Simply put, engineers use scientific knowledge to make the best use of energy and materials.

1
Who invented the hang glider?

materials ☆
- ☐ Sheet of paper
- ☐ Cellophane tape
- ☐ Paper clip
- ☐ Piece of sewing thread about 10 inches (25.4 cm) long

procedure ☆ 1. Fold the paper in half and crease it for a center line. Turn the paper so that the crease is up and fold the top corners down to form a triangle. Make sharp creases on these folds. Fasten the corners in place with a small piece of tape.

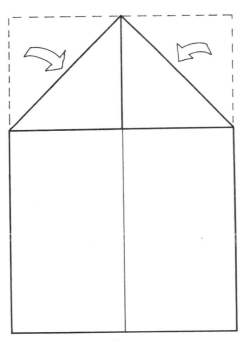

Fold the corners so that the edges meet at the center.

2. Fold the paper once more along the center crease and folded corners, then attach the paper clip about 2 inches (5 cm) back from the point, or front, of the glider. Position the paper clip so that it runs horizontally with the edge of the bottom of the glider. Fasten it in place with a small piece of tape.

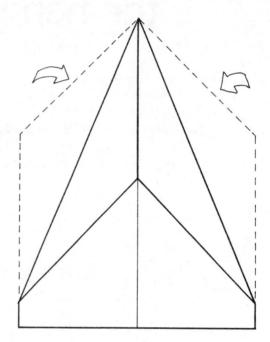

Fold the upper edges to form a sharp point.

3. Fasten one end of the thread to a point on the edge of the top of one wing about an inch from the back of the wing. Run the thread under the wing and across the bottom to the other wing. Fasten the other end of the thread with tape to an identical point on the other wing. The wings should curve in a downward sweep similar to the wings of a sea gull. Make a small slit where the thread crosses the bottom of the glider. Slide the thread in the slit. By sliding the thread from one side to the other, you can adjust the curve in the wings. Make a test flight by tossing your glider across the room. Move the paper clip forward, or back and make a test flight. What happens when you shifted the weight? Adjust the string to add more curve to one wing and flatten the other. What effect does warping the wings have?

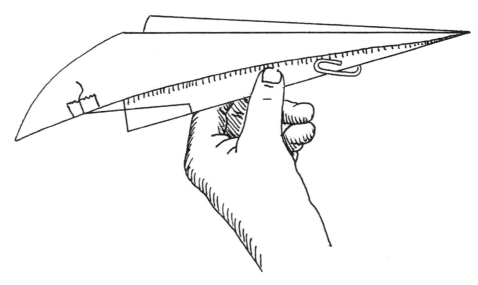

Slide the paper clip back or forward to adjust the glide angle.

results ☆ Shifting the weight forward and back caused the glider to pitch up and down. Warping the wings caused the glider to turn. Early pioneers used this method to help control their crafts.

Otto Lilienthal, from Germany, was the first man to fly repeatedly with a heavier-than-air apparatus. In 1891 he built a glider in the shape of a pair of bird's wings, with a fixed horizontal and vertical tail. It weighed about 40 pounds, was made of peeled willow rods covered with cotton fabric, and provided 107 square feet (99,403 sq. cm) of lifting surface. In the center of the wings was an opening where Otto held the glider at the height of his chest. Takeoff was accomplished by a running jump. Once in the air, he hung by his arms through two padded openings in the frame. He was able to have some control by shifting his legs and body to move the center of gravity of the glider. This apparatus was the first hang glider. He even constructed an artificial hill 50 feet (15.24 m) high to practice gliding. Otto Lilienthal made more than 2,000 flights, some longer than 900 feet (274 m) and even managed to turn in the air, before a gliding accident took his life on August 9, 1896. Reports of his flights received worldwide attention and inspired others to take up the sport of gliding.

Otto Lilienthal (1848–1896) was a German aviation pioneer. He was born May 23, 1848. After studying birds in flight, he designed and tested manned gliders. In 1891, he began flying his first successful glider and continued to make more than 2,000 flights. On August 9, 1896, Lilienthal crashed during a flight and died the following day, August 10, 1896.

Otto Lilienthal's glider was the first hang glider.

further ☆ studies
Look up Sir George Cayley in an encyclopedia. You will learn that this English gentleman experimented with gliders as early as 1808 and in 1853 one is reported to have carried his coachman on a flight of 1,500 feet (450 m). Get a book about hang gliding from your library. You will see the latest designs and learn how the newer models are much more efficient.

did you ☆
know?

❐ That under certain conditions, modern hang gliders can stay in the air as long as the pilot can endure and can travel hundreds of miles.

❐ That sky diving is a mix of hang gliding and parachuting by using a special type of parachute.

②
Who was the first to fly the Atlantic?

materials ☆
- ☐ Map of the United States
- ☐ World map or globe
- ☐ Encyclopedia

procedure ☆   1. On the map of the United States, locate San Diego, California; St. Louis, Missouri; Long Island, New York; and New York City.

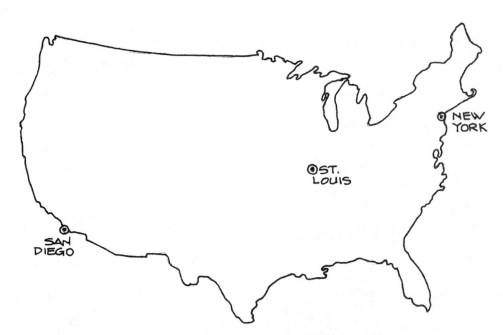

Charles Lindbergh set a coast-to-coast record in 1927, flying from San Diego to New York.

2. On the world map, locate Paris, France.

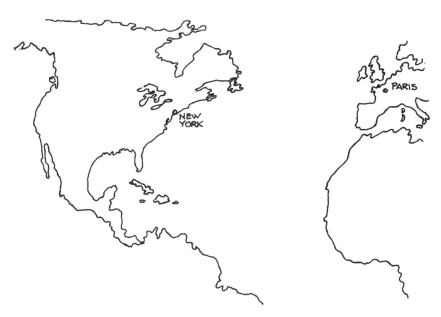

Lindbergh's transatlantic flight from New York to Paris lasted 33½ hours.

3. Look up Charles Lindbergh in the encyclopedia.

American aviator Charles A. Lindbergh (1902–1974) was the first person to fly solo nonstop across the Atlantic. He was born in Detroit on February 4, 1902, but grew up in Little Falls, Minnesota. Lindbergh learned to fly at age 20 and in 1926 was flying a mail plane between Chicago and St. Louis. He began his famous flight from New York on May 20, 1927, and 33½ hours later landed at Paris. In 1929, he married Ann Morrow Spencer. Their infant son was kidnapped and found murdered in 1932. This tragedy led to the "Lindbergh Law," which made kidnapping a federal crime. Bruno Hauptmann was convicted and executed for the crime in 1936. During World War II, Lindbergh flew 50 missions in the Pacific and later became a consultant for the U.S. space program. He died on August 26, 1974, in Hawaii.

results ☆ In 1919, Raymond Orteig, the owner of a hotel in New York City, had offered a prize of $25,000 to the pilot making the first nonstop flight from New York to Paris. Several attempts were made but all failed until 1927. Financing was provided by the citizens of St. Louis for Charles Lindbergh to have a special airplane built by the Ryan Aircraft Company in San Diego. The airplane was designed for the one purpose of lifting enough fuel to fly the Atlantic. Installing the fuel tanks caused the windshield to be eliminated, leaving only a periscope for forward visibility along with two side windows. On May 10, 1927, Lindbergh set a coast-to-coast record in the new plane, the *Spirit of St. Louis*, from San Diego to Long Island in 21 hours and 20 minutes. He stopped overnight in St. Louis. On May 20, 1927, Lindbergh took off from Roosevelt Field, New York City, at 7:52 A.M. and landed at Le Bourget Field near Paris at 10:21 P.M. the next day. His flight had covered 3,600 miles (5,792.4 km) in 33 hours, 30 minutes.

Women were active in aviation in the early years as well. The first woman to receive a pilot's license in the United States was Harriet

Harriet Quimby was a popular figure in American aviation. She performed at air shows and was the first licensed woman pilot in the United States.

Quimby, and on April 16, 1912, she became the first woman to fly across the English Channel. Tragically, a few months later Harriet crashed to her death during an air meet near Boston.

Katherine Stinson, one of the greatest of women pilots, was only 16 when she learned to fly in 1912. She also was the first woman to loop a plane and in 1918 set a U.S. distance and duration record of 601.7 miles (968.14 km) in 10 hours and 10 minutes. Katherine and her sister Marjorie also trained pilots for the Army.

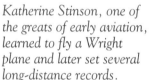

Katherine Stinson, one of the greats of early aviation, learned to fly a Wright plane and later set several long-distance records.

Jacqueline Cochran, who was raised in a foster home and left school after the third grade, received her pilot's license after only three weeks of training in 1932. She won the Bendix Transcontinental Air Race in 1938 and was voted the world's leading aviatrix in 1937, 1938, and 1939. During World War II Jacqueline Cochran organized the Women's Airforce Service Pilots (WASP) and became the first woman to ferry a bomber to England. In 1971, she was named to the Aviation Hall of Fame.

On the fifth anniversary of Lindbergh's flight, Amelia Earhart became the first woman to fly solo across the Atlantic. She flew from Harbor Grace, Newfoundland to Ireland in 1932. On May 20, 1937, Amelia Earhart and her copilot-navigator, Fred Noonan,

Jacqueline Cochran was well known in aviation circles. She held more altitude, speed, and distance records than any pilot of her time.

Amelia Earhart (1898–1937) was an American aviator. She was the first woman to make a solo flight across the Atlantic. Earhart was born on July 24, 1898, at Atchison, Kansas, and achieved fame for her flight from Newfoundland to Ireland in 1932. In July 1937, Earhart and navigator Fred Noonan attempted the first round-the-world flight following the equator. Their plane mysteriously disappeared after leaving New Guinea and a widespread search failed to find any clues to their fate.

set out from California on an eastward round-the-world flight. The flight traveled across the United States, West Africa, India, Singapore, and Australia. They disappeared at sea near tiny Howland Island in the Pacific Ocean on July 2, 1937.

further studies ☆ Look up *aviation* in an encyclopedia. See if there is a list of special days in aviation. You should find a list that shows the dates of many "firsts" in aviation history. Look in your newspaper for ads from airlines. Notice some of their daily nonstop flights and compare them to the flights of early pilots.

did you know? ☆
- ❐ That Jacqueline Cochran held more than 250 speed, distance, and altitude records, the most individual records for powered flight.
- ❐ That at the end of his flight, Lindbergh was greeted with wild enthusiasm by more than 100,000 people who had gathered at the airfield in Paris.
- ❐ That in 1954 Charles Lindbergh became a brigadier general in the Air Force Reserve.

3
Who was the first in space?

materials ☆
- ❏ String about 6 feet (1.8 m) long
- ❏ Rubber stopper from a sink or bathtub
- ❏ Barrel, or tube, from an old ballpoint pen
- ❏ Several flat metal washers
- ❏ Two large paper clips

procedure ☆
1. Tie one end of the string to the stopper and thread the other end through the barrel. Run the string through the larger opening toward the small, or pointed, end of the barrel.

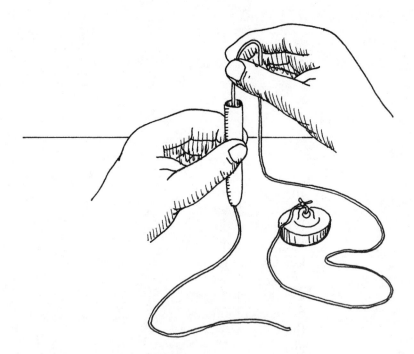

Thread the string through the barrel.

2. Thread the free end of the string through a few washers, tie a loop in the end, and attach one of the paper clips to keep the washers from falling.

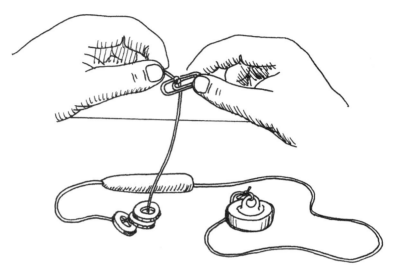

Use the paper clip to hold the washers.

3. Hold the barrel in your hand and swing the stopper in about a 3-foot (.9 m) radius. The washers should be suspended the remaining 3 feet (.9 m) below the barrel.
4. Add or subtract washers until the orbiting stopper is balanced by the washers.

results ☆ In your experiment, the weight of the washers supplied centripetal force. In space, gravity supplies the centripetal force to keep small bodies in orbit around larger bodies. Centrifugal force created by the movement of a satellite tries to make it leave its orbit. Centripetal force tries to keep the satellite in orbit.

On April 12, 1961, Lieutenant Yuri A. Gagarin, a 27-year-old Soviet cosmonaut became the world's first man to fly in space. The flight lasted 1 hour and 48 minutes, orbiting the earth once at an altitude of 112 to 203 miles (180.2 to 326.6 km). Following reentry, Gagarin ejected at 22,000 feet (6,705.6 m) and landed in a pasture. On May 5, 1961, Alan B. Shepard, a 37-year-old Navy commander, became the first American in space with a flight lasting 15 minutes at an altitude of 125 miles (201.1 km).

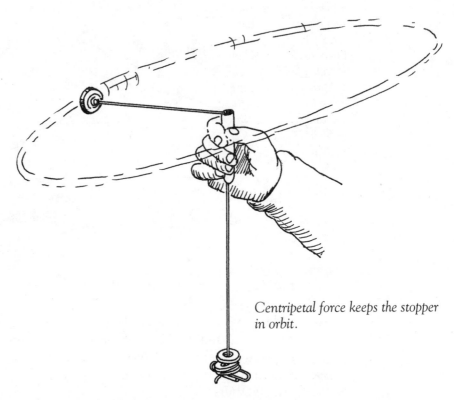

Centripetal force keeps the stopper in orbit.

On June 27, 1983, Sally Ride became the first American woman in space. She was one of five astronauts launched aboard the Shuttle Challenger on a six-day flight. In October 1984, she went into space a second time on a mission during which Kathryn Sullivan became the first American woman to walk in space.

On the third Challenger flight in August 1983, Lieutenant Colonel Guion Stewart Bluford became the first black American astronaut. Guion Bluford studied aerospace engineering at Pennsylvania State University where he graduated in 1964. He joined the U.S. Air Force and saw extensive combat service in Vietnam. In 1978, Bluford received his doctorate in aerospace engineering and was accepted into the astronaut program that year.

Yuri Gagarin (1934–1968) was a Soviet cosmonaut who was the first man in space. He was born on March 9, 1934. He was a jet pilot in the air force and was selected to be in the Soviet space program in March 1960. Gagarin was launched into space on April 12, 1961, and orbited the earth once. Parades and world tours followed his successful flight and he began training for the next manned space flight. He was killed when his MiG jet crashed in 1968.

Alan Shepard (1923–) was the first American in space. He was born on November 18, 1923, at East Derry, New Hampshire. Shepard graduated from the U.S. Naval Academy in 1944 and became a test pilot in 1950. In 1959, he was one of the first seven men chosen to train as astronauts. Shepard made his first flight on May 5, 1961, and his second and last flight from January 31 to February 9, 1971, during which he and Edgar Mitchell spent 33 hours on the moon. Shepard retired as a rear admiral in 1974.

Who was the first in space? **21**

Sally Ride (1951–) was the first American woman astronaut. She was born on May 26, 1951, at Encino, California, and in 1977 received a Ph.D. in physics from Stanford University. Ride flew on shuttle missions in 1983 and 1984, and in 1986, she was a member of the commission that investigated the Challenger tragedy. She became the director of the Space Institute of the University of California in 1989.

Guion Stewart Bluford received a doctorate in aerospace engineering from the Air Force Institute of Technology and acted as mission specialist on the third flight of the space shuttle Challenger.

Place a glass of water on the floor and lie across a chair so that your stomach is higher than your mouth. Try to drink the water. Notice how difficult it is. Now use a straw. It is still not easy because of gravity. In space, astronauts have to use plastic bottles and bags. Squeezing the bottles with their hands provides the necessary pressure to move the food to their mouths.

did you ☆
know?

❑ That if the air in a spacecraft was not circulated by fans, the astronauts could suffocate in their own breath. The carbon dioxide from their breath would stay near their face and be breathed again, something like putting your head in a plastic bag.

❑ That without gravity, body fluids do not drain as they should. Because of this, astronauts often have symptoms of a cold: runny nose, fluids in the chest, and a loss of senses of smell and taste.

4
Who invented the lever and the screw?

- ☐ Heavy desk or table
- ☐ Two boards about the same height of the table
- ☐ Pencil
- ☐ Colored marker
- ☐ Sheet of paper
- ☐ Scissors

procedure ☆

1. A *lever* is a stiff bar that turns around a pivotal point called a *fulcrum*. The advantage is in the short distance between the load and the fulcrum, and a long distance between the fulcrum and the point where the effort is applied. To make a lever, place one of the boards on its end next to the table, and the other board on top. With one end of the board under the edge of the table, press down on the other end. Is the heavy table easy to lift?

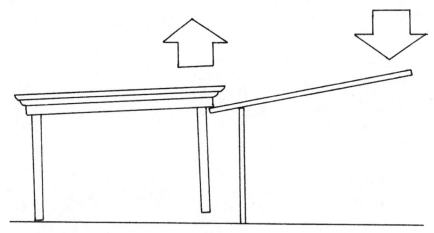

A lever can be used to lift a heavy object.

2. A *screw* is really an inclined plane, or ramp, that is formed into a spiral. Cut a right triangle from the sheet of paper to make a ramp. Always cut away from yourself. Use a marker to color the cut edge. Roll the paper on the pencil from the short side of the triangle to the point. Keep the bottom, or base line, of the triangle even as it rolls. What pattern does the marked edge form?

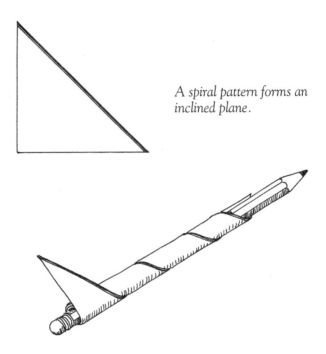

A spiral pattern forms an inclined plane.

results ☆ When you pressed down on the end of the board, the table was easily lifted off the floor. This type of lever is called a *first-class* lever because the fulcrum is between the effort and the load. In a *second-class* lever, the load is between the fulcrum and the effort. A wheelbarrow is a second-class lever. A *third-class* lever places the effort between the fulcrum and the load. Your forearm is a third-class lever. Around 200 B.C. Archimedes, a Greek mathematician and inventor, discovered the laws of the lever and invented the Archimedean screw. The screw was used to draw water from ships and to raise water to irrigate fields.

Archimedes (298–212 B.C.) was a Greek
mathematician who developed the theory of levers
and pulleys and invented a device to pump water,
which was called the Archimedes screw. He is also
credited with inventing the catapult and a burning
mirror for the defense of his native Syracuse.
Archimedes made many contributions to geometry,
laid the foundation for calculus, and developed an
approximation of pi. He is probably best known for
his studies on the weight of a body immersed in a
liquid (see experiment 22). These studies led him to
propose what is called the Archimedes principle.
According to legend, Archimedes ran naked
down a street crying "Eureka, I have found
it" after making his discovery while taking a bath.
He was killed when the Romans invaded
Syracuse in 212 B.C.

**further ☆
studies**

Move the fulcrum of your lever to see how it changes the effort to
lift a load. Notice that the closer the fulcrum is to the load, the
less effort is required. If you pull a nail from a board with a claw
hammer, are you using a lever? Is a bottle opener a lever? How
many places can you find where an inclined plane, or screw is used
to reduce effort? Are driveways inclined planes?

**did you ☆
know?**

❑ That the lever and screw is really a simple machine, because a
machine is any device that does work.
❑ That Archimedes made this boast about levers: "Give me a
place to stand on, and I will move the earth."

5
Who invented the steam engine?

materials   ❏ 2 feet (182.88 cm) of ⅛-inch (.3175-cm) copper tubing
    (available at most hardware stores)
❏ Pencil or ballpoint pen
❏ 9-inch (22.86-cm) aluminum pie pan
❏ Sink or bathtub
❏ Stub of a candle

procedure   1. The copper tubing is soft, so carefully bend the middle of the
    tube about six times around the pencil to form a small, tight
    coil. Now you need to bend the tubing into a base. With the
    coil hanging down, start from each side of the coil, come out

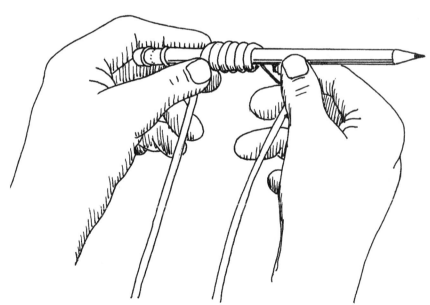

Form the copper tubing into a coil.

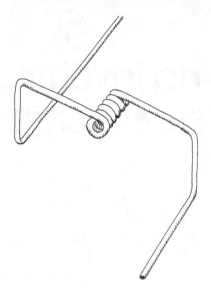

Carefully shape the tube to fit the pan.

about 2 inches (5.08 cm) and bend the tubing down. Next, move down the tubing about 3 inches (7.62 cm) and bend one tube back horizontal, and parallel the coil. Bend the other tube back horizontal in the other direction. The coil should now be able to stand supported by the tubing. There must be enough room to fit the candle under the coil.

2. Place the tubing in the center of the pie pan and bend the ends of the tubing up over the lip of the pan and back down. Now bend the ends of the tubing horizontally in opposite directions.

Make sure the coil is full of water; then light the candle.

The final bends are to be the exhaust of the engine. Making the tubing fit the pan is a little tricky; just take your time and make dry runs to be sure the ends of the tubing stick down below the pan and back in opposite directions.

3. While filling the sink with water, run water in one end of the tubing to be sure the coil is full of water. When the sink is full, float the pan in the water and place the tubing in the pan. Make sure the ends of the tubing is well under water.

4. Ask an adult for permission to light the candle. Place the candle under the coil.

results ☆ In a few minutes the pan will start to rotate and you should be able to see ripples, indicating tiny puffs of water coming from the ends of the copper tubes. The flame from the candle heats the water in the coil, turning it into steam. The steam forces water from the ends of the tubes, causing the pan to spin. The pulses of water are caused when the steam condenses and is pulled back into the coil to be heated again. The copper tubing will get very hot, so allow it to cool before handling it.

The first successful steam engines were developed in the 1600s when steam was used to drain water from mines. In 1712, English

James Watt (1736–1819) was born in Greenock, Scotland, on January 19, 1736. In 1776, he was employed by the University of Glasgow, where he became interested in steam power. Watt immigrated to Birmingham, England, in 1774 and formed a partnership with Matthew Boulton to develop and manufacture steam engines. He retired in 1790 and died on August 25, 1819.

blacksmith Thomas Newcomen invented a more practical steam engine consisting of a horizontal beam balanced in the middle with a cylinder connected to one end. James Watt experimented with steam engines and took out his first patent in 1769. Although he didn't invent the steam engine, he made many improvements that allowed them to be used for other purposes than pumping water.

further studies ☆ In your experiment, the pan just spun in circles. If you had used a narrow bread pan and pointed the exhausts in the same direction, would you have a steamboat? Could your steam engine turn a wheel or paddle? Could a magnifying glass be used to heat the coil?

did you know? ☆ ❏ That Hero, an early scientist in Egypt, described the first steam engine in 120 B.C. However, it performed no useful work.

The first steam engine performed no work.

❐ That steam turbines were invented in the late 1800s, and were used to turn the propellers of ocean liners as well as huge generators at electric plants.

❐ That in 1878, black inventor and mechanical engineer Granville T. Woods was an engineer on the British steamer *Ironsides*, and in 1880 was handling steam locomotives. Woods, a prolific inventor, patented 23 separate inventions.

Granville T. Woods received some 50 patents during his lifetime, and during the 20 years between 1879 and 1899, he patented 23 separate inventions. In one year, 1887, he registered seven separate inventions of an ingenious railway communications system he devised.

6
Who invented the diesel engine?

materials ☆ ❏ Tire pump
❏ Flat tire or basketball

procedure ☆ 1. Operate the pump to inflate the tire.

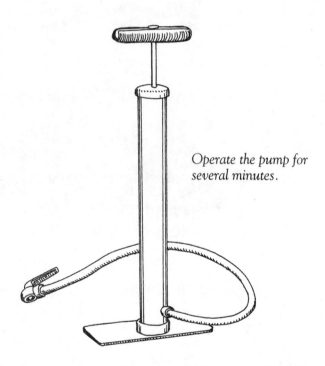

Operate the pump for several minutes.

2. After several minutes of hard pumping, feel the lower part of the barrel of the pump. Feel the hose connected to the tire.

Rudolf Diesel (1858–1913) was born in Germany on March 18, 1858. He became an engineer and inventor and developed a type of internal-combustion engine that burned fuel oil. The ignition of his engine was brought about by heat resulting from air compression, instead of an electric spark, as in gasoline engines of that time. On September 29, 1913, Diesel disappeared from a boat while crossing the English Channel and was never seen again.

results ☆ The lower part of the pump and connecting hose should feel very warm. The heat generated is produced by compressing the air. When molecules of air are pressed closer together, they are forced to rub and strike each other more than normal. This rubbing and striking caused by compressing produces heat. In your experiment, you were able to compress the air enough to generate a small amount of heat. If air confined in a cylinder is suddenly compressed, the air gets hotter. In a diesel engine, each piston compresses air in a cylinder. Fuel is injected into the cylinders and the air is hot enough to ignite it. The explosion forces the pistons to move, providing power.

German mechanical engineer Rudolf Diesel developed an internal-combustion machine that used oil as a fuel. The engine ignited the oil–air mixture by the heat developed through compression. He patented his design for the engine in 1892 and by 1897 had operated the first successful diesel engine.

further studies ☆ Diesel engines normally sound different than gasoline engines. The next time you see a large truck, notice if it has a diesel engine. Many cars and small trucks also use diesel engines. Do you think it is practical for farm and heavy equipment operators to use diesel power? Why isn't diesel power used in airplanes? Are diesel engines heavier?

did you ☆ know?

☐ That Rudolf Diesel mysteriously disappeared from a German ship while he was traveling to London. He was never found.

☐ That Diesel built his first engine in 1893. It exploded and he was nearly killed.

7
Who invented the electric motor?

materials ❑ Cardboard support
❑ Pencil
❑ One solid copper wire about 8 inches (20.32 cm) long
❑ Flashlight battery
❑ Two small copper wires, each about 2 feet (60.96 cm) long
❑ Horseshoe magnet

procedure ✮ 1. Fold the ends of the cardboard up to make a support for the pencil. Press the pencil through each side of the cardboard folds near the top.
2. Bend the short piece of copper wire into a U shape, with the ends bent out about ¼ inch (.635 cm). Tie the ends of the two copper wires to the short bends in the copper U. Loop the wires over the pencil a couple of times so that copper U is suspended from the pencil like a swing.
3. Place the horseshoe magnet on its edge so that the copper U is free to swing between the poles of the magnet.
4. Connect the free ends of the copper wire to the battery.

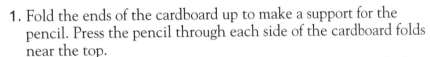

Place the copper U between the two poles of the magnet.

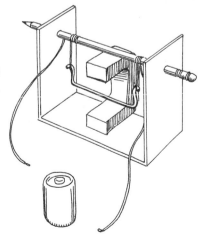

results ☆ The copper U will swing out or in depending on which way the battery was connected. When the electrical current flows through the copper U, it becomes an electromagnet and is attracted or repelled from the magnet. This principle is what makes a motor work.

In 1821, Michael Faraday, an English chemist and physicist, built an apparatus that demonstrated that electromagnetic effects can produce motion. He positioned a magnet with one end exposed in a cup of mercury. A wire was suspended from above until it touched the mercury. A battery was connected between the mercury and the other end of the wire. The free end of the wire immediately began to whirl around the magnet. He had invented the electromagnetic motor. It occurred to Faraday that if electricity could produce magnetism, couldn't magnetism produce electricity?

Michael Faraday (1791–1867) was born at Newington, Surrey, near London on September 22, 1791, and received only a basic education. He was apprenticed to a bookbinder at age 14, where he developed an interest in physics and chemistry. Faraday became one of the greatest English chemists and physicists, and in 1831, he demonstrated electromagnetic induction, the principle of the electric motor. He held a position at the Royal Institute in London for 54 years. Faraday died on August 25, 1867.

further ☆ Swap the connections to the battery. What happens? Does the
studies direction of the current affect the movement of the copper U? To
keep the copper U swinging, would the connections need to be
constantly, and quickly switched?

did you ☆ ❒ That Michael Faraday became a popular speaker and developed
know? a special series of scientific lectures for children. They were
delivered each Christmas for many years and continued to be
shown on television.

❒ That in 1881, the First International Electrical Congress called
the standard unit of capacitance the *farad*, for Michael Faraday.
A capacitor consists of two metal plates separated by an
insulator. The capacitance, or size, of a capacitor is measured in
farads.

8
Who invented
alternating current?

materials ☆
- ❒ Piece of cardboard, 3 × 4 inches (7.62 × 10.16 cm)
- ❒ Insulated wire (bell wire), about 20 feet (6.1 meters)
- ❒ Insulated wire (bell wire), about 10 feet (3 meters)
- ❒ Wire strippers
- ❒ Bar magnet
- ❒ Magnetic compass

procedure ☆

1. Fold two ends of the cardboard up to form supports for the wire. Wrap the longer wire around the cardboard about 20 times. Leave about 12 inches (30.48 cm) of surplus wire for connections. Have an adult strip about 1 inch (2.54 cm) of the insulation from each end. Place the compass on the cardboard and inside the coil of wire.
2. Wrap the shorter wire around your fingers about 20 times to make a coil slightly larger than the bar magnet. Leave the free ends to make connections to the coil around the cardboard. Have an adult strip about 1 inch (2.54 cm) of the insulation from each end to make the connections. Twist the bare ends together to connect this coil to the coil around the cardboard.
3. Move the bar magnet abruptly in and then out of the center of the smaller coil and watch the needle on the compass.

results ☆ When the magnet was first pushed into the coil, the needle is deflected in one direction and then in the opposite direction when the magnet was removed. The deflection of the needle indicates that a small electrical current was flowing. When the needle changed directions it indicated that the electrical current had flowed in the other direction. When an electrical current flows first in one direction then the other in cycles it is called *alternating current*.

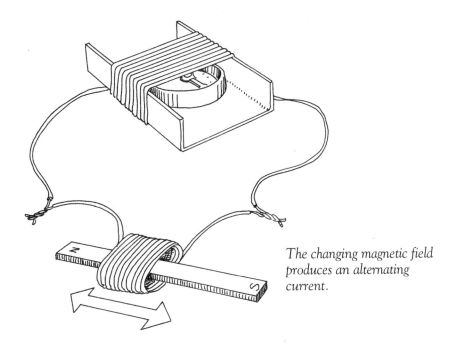

The changing magnetic field produces an alternating current.

Based on Faraday's experiments, other scientists begin constructing hand-cranked generators. These generators operated by moving a coil back and forth in front of a magnet or by moving a magnet inside a coil. Today's generators use a rotary motion between the coil and the magnet instead of the back and forth motion. In 1832, Hippolyte Pixii, a French instrument maker, built the first apparatus that had fixed coils wound on a U-shaped iron rod. Above the rod a horseshoe magnet was attached to a shaft driven by a hand crank. When the handle was turned, the rotating magnet produced an alternating electric current in the coils. Pixii's machine, which he created after reading papers on Faraday's work, was the forerunner of the generators we use today. However, at the time there was no use for alternating current.

further ☆ studies
Transformers can be used to raise or lower the voltage or current of an alternating electrical current. The nature of electricity dictates that voltage is easier to move than current. This means that transmission lines carry a very high voltage with a lower current. Notice the electric company's substations in your area. These are

transformers that reduce the voltage down to a more usable voltage. Notice the transmission lines coming into the substation. Compare the size of these lines to the ones near your home. Must wires be larger to carry more electricity? Electric companies cannot store electricity. They must anticipate the public's need and produce the energy on demand. At any one moment about 2,000 thunderstorms might be happening around the world producing 100 lightning strikes each second. If this energy could be captured and stored, could lightning be a source of electricity in the future? If we could harness the energy from lightning, several hundred million dollars in damages and about 10,000 forest fires could be saved each year in the United States alone.

did you ☆ know?

- ❏ That direct current lightning for example occurs in nature but alternating current was invented for better control of this energy.
- ❏ That some cross-country transmission lines carry up to 760,000 volts.
- ❏ That some electric power plants produce more than 2 million kilowatts of electricity.

Part 2
The young astronomer

Astronomy is the study of heavenly bodies and their movements. Hundreds of years ago it was believed that the earth was the center of the universe and the sun, moon, and stars moved around it once every day. Today we know that the earth is a planet that moves around the sun. The sun is a star and our star system, or galaxy, has about 100,000 million stars. Our sun appears much larger and hotter than the other stars only because it is closer. It is about 93 million miles from the earth. Because of the vastness of space, instead of miles, astronomers use the distance light travels in one year, a little less than 6 million million miles. This distance is called a *light-year*. The nearest bright star, except for the sun, is Alpha Centauri. It is about 4.31 light-years away. This means that it takes the light from this star more than four years to reach us. It also means that what we see in the universe is old news. If you could sit on a star 100 light-years away with a huge telescope, you could see life as it was in the 1890s. Railroads had crossed the

United States. Pioneers were taming the west, and "horseless carriages" chugged and snorted over unpaved roads. When we look at the stars, we look back in time.

To begin the study of this exciting science you need only good eyes and a dark night. Later you might need binoculars or a telescope and even experiment with a camera.

9
Who first suggested that the earth revolves around the sun?

materials ☆
- ❐ Small lamp without the shade
- ❐ Ball or globe for the earth
- ❐ Map of the world

procedure ☆ 1. Use the lamp to represent the sun and the ball to represent the earth. Look at the map to find the latitude where you live. Draw a circle around the ball to represent the latitude, then mark an X for your location. The top and bottom of the ball represent the north and south axis.

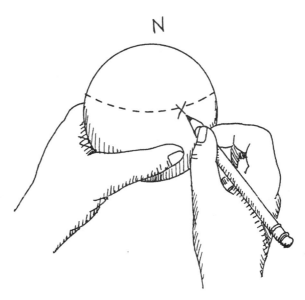

Mark your latitude on the ball.

2. Hold the ball with the north–south axis straight up and down. Now tilt the top of the ball about 23 degrees to the right to represent the tilt of the earth.
3. Hold the ball a few feet (a meter or so) from, and on the same level with, the lamp. Slowly rotate the ball counterclockwise and move it in a circle around the lamp. One complete circle represents one year. Stop at four equal spaces in the circle and notice how the shadow on the ball moves.

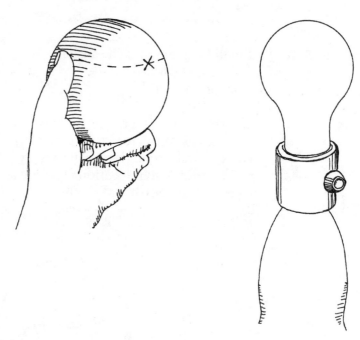

Watch the shadow change as the ball circles the lamp.

results ☆ The four equal spaces represent the seasons: autumn, winter, spring, and summer. Notice how the lengths of the days changed at your location. This change happens because, during half of the year, the North Pole is tilted toward the sun. At this time of year in the Northern Hemisphere, the days are longer than 12 hours. This time is the spring and summer. During the other half of the year, the North Pole is tilted away from the sun. The days are shorter and the nights longer. This time is autumn and winter in the Northern Hemisphere. Notice that the seasons are opposite in the Southern Hemisphere.

About 360 B.C., the Greek philosopher Eudoxus developed a plan that showed the earth motionless and at the center of the universe. Later, another philosopher, Aristarchus, proposed that the movements of the heavens could be explained if the earth moved around the sun. But his ideas were considered ridiculous. In 1543, Polish astronomer Nicolaus Copernicus published a book that supported the idea that the earth and other planets revolved around the sun. But few people accepted his theory until 1687, when Isaac Newton published the law of universal gravitation, which explained why the planets moved around the sun.

Nicolaus Copernicus (1473–1543) was born February 19, 1473, in Torn, Poland. The son of a prosperous merchant, he studied at the University of Krakow and other universities and later became a canon in the church. His main interest was astronomy. Copernicus demonstrated that the sun, not the earth, was the center of our solar system. He realized that what people saw in the heavens was affected by the earth's movement and not the other way around. He died on May 24, 1543.

further studies ☆ If the earth's axis were straight up and down, would the seasons change? Can you see why Alaska is sometimes called the "land of the midnight sun"?

did you know? ☆ ❑ That, fearing ridicule, Copernicus delayed publishing his book until he was near the end of his life.

❏ That no one knows quite how or why gravity works, but everything in the universe exerts its own gravitational pull on everything else.

❏ That gravity is a really a weak force but can be felt over enormous distances. The immense gravitational pull of our sun is the force that holds the nine planets, including the earth, in our solar system.

10
Who discovered the laws of falling bodies?

❏ Softball
❏ Golf ball
❏ High platform (upstairs window or porch)
❏ Two sheets of paper the same size

procedure ☆ 1. Get an adult to help you. Take the balls to a high platform.
Make sure the area is clear below you. Hold the balls at the
same level and release them at the same time. Which ball hits
the ground first?

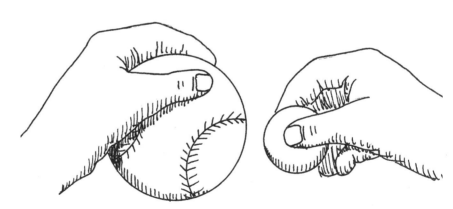

Drop both balls at the same time.

2. Crumple one of the sheets of paper into a ball and drop both
pieces at the same time. Which one hits the ground first?

results ☆ Both balls strike the ground at the same time even though the golf
ball is lighter. The force of gravity pulls on all bodies alike,

regardless of shape, size, or density. In a vacuum, a feather and a bowling ball will fall at the same speed. The ball of paper falls much faster than the sheet of paper, even though both pieces of paper weigh the same. The sheet of paper is slowed by the resistance of the air.

About the end of the 1500s, Galileo proposed the law of falling bodies. He devised experiments to show that gravity makes all freely falling objects drop at the same constant acceleration, regardless of how much they weigh. The acceleration of gravity is expressed in terms of the rate of increase of velocity per second. On Earth the standard is 32.17 feet (980.665 cm) per second per second. The velocity increases 32.17 feet per second for each second of the fall. For example, at the end of the first second, the velocity would be 32.17 feet per second; at the end of the second second, it would be 64.34 feet per second; and at the end of the third second it would be 64.34 plus 32.17, or 96.51 feet per second. The object will continue to fall faster until the resistance of the air balances the pull of gravity. The object will then fall at the same speed, called *terminal velocity*.

Galileo Galilei (1564–1642), known mostly by his first name, was born in Pisa, Italy, and studied medicine at a local university. But he soon became more interested in science and was the first astronomer to use a telescope. Galileo disagreed with the sciences of that time and, according to legend, dropped weights from the leaning tower of Pisa to prove his theory of falling bodies. Because of his views, he was forced to leave Pisa in 1591. On January 10, 1610, Galileo discovered four satellites, or moons, orbiting Jupiter and published opinions supporting the Copernicus theory. These views were contrary to the teachings of the church, and Galileo lived the last eight years of his life under house arrest near Florence. He became blind in 1637 but remained active until he died on January 8, 1642. About 340 years later, the Roman Catholic church officially accepted Galileo's teachings; he was finally pardoned by Pope John II.

further studies ☆ If you multiply 32.17 by the number of seconds of a falling body, would you get the velocity of the body? How fast would it be falling after 10 seconds? Would the terminal velocity of a skydiver be slowed if the diver's arms and legs were spread out and the skydiver was falling horizontally? What would happen if the arms and legs were pulled in and the body was positioned in a dive?

did you know? ☆

❑ That, because of the differences in gravitational pull, if you could jump 6 feet (1.83 m) high on earth, you could jump 36 feet (10.97 m) high on the moon, but only 2.5 feet (76.2 cm) on Jupiter.

❑ That in 1929, Albert Einstein said that gravitation and electromagnetism might be related.

Albert Einstein (1879–1955) was born on March 14, 1879, in Ulm, Germany. He is considered one of the greatest scientists of all time. Einstein is best known for his theory of relativity, which he first proposed in 1905 when he was only 26. In the 1930s, Einstein fled Nazi Germany and accepted a position to direct the school of mathematics at the Institute for Advanced Study in Princeton, New Jersey. He died at Princeton on April 18, 1955.

11
Who first tried to determine the size of heavenly bodies?

materials ☆
- ❏ 3-x-5-inch (7.62-x-12.7-cm) index card
- ❏ Tape measure
- ❏ Hobby knife
- ❏ Long support, 6-foot (1.83-meter) fishing pole
- ❏ Cellophane tape
- ❏ Know the distance to the moon—240,000 miles (384,000 km)
- ❏ Night with a full moon

procedure ☆

1. With the hobby knife, cut a square in the center of the card. Be careful to cut away from yourself. Make each side of the square exactly ½ inch (1.27 cm) long.

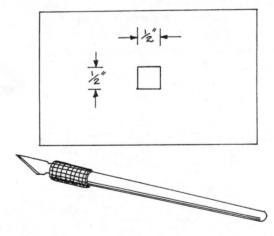

Carefully cut a square in the card.

2. Tape the card to the end of the support and fold it so that it stands upright.

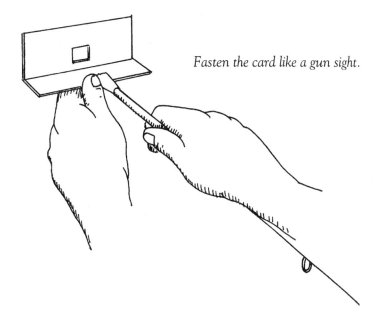

Fasten the card like a gun sight.

3. Aim the support at the moon. Sight along the support and move your head back away from the card until the diameter of the moon just fills the ½ inch (1.27 cm) square. Make a mark on the support even with your eye.
4. Measure the distance from the mark to the card.

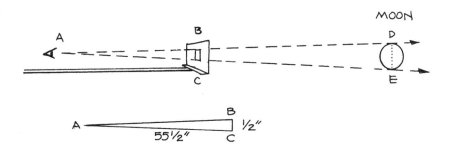

Measure the distance to the card to calculate the diameter of the moon.

results ☆ You have constructed two triangles that will allow you to calculate the diameter of the moon. The distance between the mark and the card should be about 55½ inches (140.97 cm). The opening in the card is ½ inch (1.27 cm). If you divide 55½ inches by ½ inch (1.27 cm) you get the number 111. The distance to the moon is about 240,000 miles (384,000 km). By dividing 240,000 miles (384,000 km) by the ratio 111 from the first triangle you find the approximate diameter of the moon, 2,162 miles (3,459.46 km). Do not try this experiment on the sun. The sun's rays can damage your eyes very quickly. About 280 B.C., the Greek astronomer Aristarchus used the shadow of the earth cast on the moon and mathematics to estimate that the moon had a diameter about one-third that of the earth. Later he used a right triangle and measured the angles to determine the diameter of the moon. His calculations were correct, but he lacked instruments to make accurate measurements.

further studies ☆ Hold a ball up in front of you at arm's length. Ask someone to stand several feet (a couple of meters) away and shine a flashlight on the ball. The ball will represent the moon, your head will be the earth, and the flashlight will be the sun. Slowly turn in a circle and you will see that we always see the same side of the moon. From the sun, could you see all sides of the moon?

did you know? ☆
❐ That the moon travels around the earth at an average speed of 2,300 miles per hour (3,700 km per hour).
❐ That a day on the moon would last about two weeks.
❐ That the moon has mountain ranges with peaks over 25,000 feet (7,620 m).

12
Who was the first to draw a map of the sky?

materials ☆
- ☐ Tin can
- ☐ Paper
- ☐ Pencil
- ☐ Two or three different-sized nails
- ☐ Hammer
- ☐ Dark room
- ☐ Flashlight

procedure ☆

1. Find a clean, empty can that doesn't have any sharp edges. Place the can on the paper and mark a circle around the edge of the can.
2. Draw a constellation (the Big Dipper, for example) inside the circle. Mark the stars heavily so that you can see them through the back of the paper.
3. Turn the paper over and place it on the bottom of the can. Ask an adult to make holes in the can using the hammer and nails. Use different-sized nails to show the different brightness of each star.

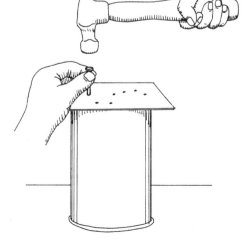

Use a larger nail to show the brighter stars.

4. Remove the paper and take the can to a dark room. Place the flashlight inside the can and shine it on the ceiling.

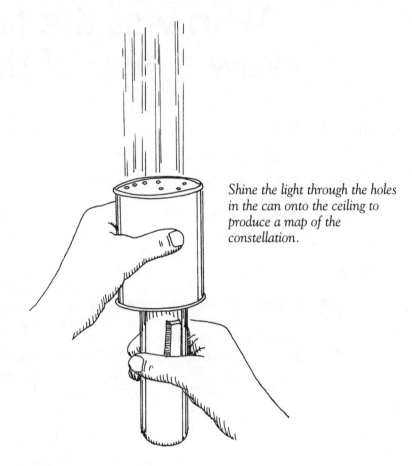

Shine the light through the holes in the can onto the ceiling to produce a map of the constellation.

results ☆ You will see a star map of your constellation on the ceiling. About 350 B.C., the Greek mathematician Eudoxus was the first to attempt a map of the sky. To locate the stars without landmarks, he drew imaginary grid lines that we now call longitude and latitude.

further ☆ Look up *astronomy* in an encyclopedia and find maps of the
studies constellations. It should show the times of the year that different constellations can be seen. This is one of the best ways to become familiar with the night sky.

❏ That in 1928, the International Astronomical Union officially recognized 88 constellations.

❏ That by knowing the constellations, you can locate stars, planets, and even comets.

13
Who was the first to accurately estimate the size of the solar system?

materials ☆ ❏ Table
❏ Yardstick
❏ Two thumbtacks
❏ Seven straight pins
❏ Nine small strips of paper
❏ Pencil
❏ Round dish or pan

procedure ☆

1. Write the names of the planets on the strips of paper. Mercury, Venus, Earth, Mars, Jupiter, Saturn, Uranus, Neptune, and Pluto. Place the dish upside down on the table. Extend the yardstick flat on the table and straight out from the dish.
2. Measure out from the dish just a little less than ½ inch (1.27 cm). Use a pin to fasten the paper marked Mercury to the yardstick. Come out to the ¾-inch (1.9-cm) mark and pin the paper marked Venus. Pin the paper marked Earth at the 1-inch (2.54-cm) mark. The paper marked Mars should be pinned at the 1½-inch (3.8-cm) mark.
3. Use a thumbtack to mark Jupiter at the 5½-inch (13.97-cm) mark. Use the other thumbtack to mark Saturn at the 9½-inch (24.13-cm) mark.
4. Use a pin to mark Uranus at the 19½-inch (49.53-cm) mark. Pin the paper marked Neptune at the 30-inch (76.2-cm) mark, and place the paper marked Pluto about 3½ inches (8.89 cm) past the end of the yardstick. Pluto should be about 39½ inches (100.33 cm) from the edge of the dish.

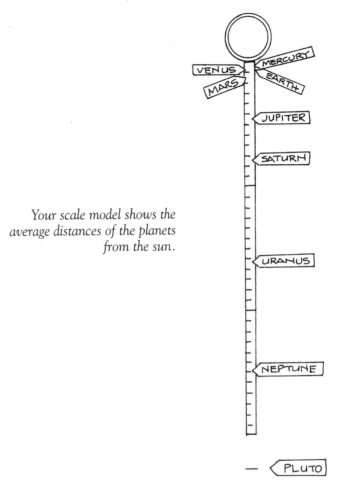

Your scale model shows the average distances of the planets from the sun.

results ☆ You now have a rough scale model of the average distances each planet is from the sun. You have used a unit of measurement called the *astronomical unit*. An astronomical unit is the average distance between Earth and the Sun, a little less than 93 million miles (148.8 million km). In your experiment, 1 inch (2.54 cm) represented 1 astronomical unit. The thumbtacks represented the two largest planets, Jupiter and Saturn.

In 1672, French astronomer Gian Domenico Cassini in Paris and astronomer Jean Richer on the northern shore of South America worked out the angles of Mars. By using the angles from these two positions, Cassini was able to calculate the distance to Mars. From these figures he could calculate the size of the solar system. From your experiment, you can see just how small we and our world are in comparison.

further ☆ studies
Instead of using 1 inch (2.54 cm) for an astronomical unit, imagine how far Pluto would be if you used 1 mile (1.6 km). Now imagine 93 million miles (148.8 million km) as an astronomical unit.

did you ☆ know?
❑ That Earth has a diameter of almost 8,000 miles (12,800 km), compared to Jupiter's nearly 89,000 miles (142,400 km) and Saturn's 74,000 miles (118,400 km).

❑ That Mars has the largest known volcano. This volcano, Olympus Mons, is about 15 miles (24 km) high, three times higher than Mount Everest.

14
Who was the first to detect a double star?

materials ☆
- ❏ Magnetic compass
- ❏ Clear night
- ❏ Binoculars or telescope

procedure ☆
1. Face the northern half of the sky and locate the Big and Little Dippers. The end star in the handle of the Little Dipper is the North Star. Both groups of stars form the outlines of long-handled cups.
2. Locate the handle of the Big Dipper. Find the next to the last star in the handle. The name of this star is Mizar. Look closely at Mizar with the binoculars or telescope.

results ☆
You might have been able to see that Mizar has a companion star. It is called Alcor. Together they make up a double star.

In 1650, Italian astronomer John Baptist Riccioli was the first to detect a double star—it was Mizar.

further studies ☆
Look at the night sky without trying to focus on any of the stars. Let your eyes drift until you notice a particular bright star. You should also see several dim stars surrounding the bright star. Look at one of the dim stars. It will probably disappear. Look back at the bright star and the dim star should reappear. When you want to see a dim star, don't look directly at it.

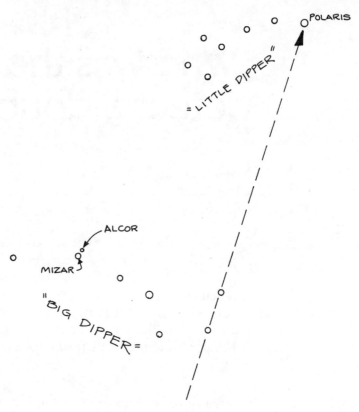

Mizar and Alcor make up a double star.

did you ☆ know?

❑ That a double star is a pair of stars which revolve around a center of gravity between them.

❑ That the light that you see from the Big Dipper is 70 or 80 years old.

Part 3
The young chemist

Chemistry is the science that deals with the makeup of materials and the reactions and changes in these materials. Chemical reactions occur all around us, all the time. When a piece of metal rusts, when burning wood turns to ash, even when you make a piece of toast. In ancient times, chemistry was the work of alchemists, who were concerned mostly with trying to turn cheaper metals into gold.

As in most sciences, early chemists were almost always men, but in the late 1800s, Ellen Swallow Richards became the first American woman to attend a scientific college, the Massachusetts Institute of Technology (M.I.T.). She received her bachelor of science degree in 1873 and became the first student to earn a doctorate in chemistry; however, she was denied the honor because the all-male faculty would not award its first doctorate to a woman. In 1876, Ellen Richards became the first woman to teach at

Ellen Swallow Richards graduated from Vassar College in 1870 and the Massachusetts Institute of Technology in 1873. She was a pioneer in the scientific analysis of household management and coined the term home economics.

M.I.T., where she created the first woman's science laboratory in the world. In 1899, she started the home economics movement.

Today's chemists are well-trained men and women who conduct exciting research and develop new products. Chemistry has also affected medicine, because it is responsible for the discovery of new drugs and medicines. Our lives today and in the future would be very different without chemists and chemistry.

15
Who first defined
an element?

materials ☆ ❑ Pan
❑ Water
❑ Stove

procedure ☆ 1. Ask an adult for permission to use the stove. Fill the pan with tap water.

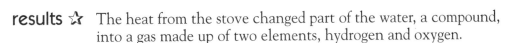

2. Heat the water just long enough for it to start to boil. You can see gases forming. Be careful because the escaping gases can cause severe burns.

results ☆ The heat from the stove changed part of the water, a compound, into a gas made up of two elements, hydrogen and oxygen.

Robert Boyle (1627–1691) was born on January 25, 1627, and died December 30, 1691. He was a British chemist and physicist and is often referred to as the father of chemistry. He taught that elements are simple bodies that combine to form compounds. He studied the compression and expansion of air and other gases and formulated Boyle's law relating the volume of a gas to its pressure.

Aristotle believed there were four elements: earth, water, fire, and air. That theory was accepted for about 2,000 years. In 1661, the British scientist Robert Boyle published a book that suggested that an element was a simple component that could not be changed into anything simpler. Anything that could be changed into something simpler was not an element.

Everything is either an element, a compound of elements, or a mixture of a variety of compounds and elements.

further ☆ studies
Place a glass of ice water on a paper towel and let it sit for a few minutes. Do water droplets form on the outside of the glass? Does air contain the elements oxygen and hydrogen? What other elements make up air? Is nitrogen an element?

did you ☆ know?
❑ That under ordinary conditions, two elements are liquids, 11 elements are gases, and the rest are solids.
❑ That sugar tastes sweet, but is made up of three elements that have no taste at all.
❑ That table salt is made up of two elements that are very poisonous—sodium and chlorine.

16
Who invented carbonated water?

materials ☆
- ❑ Drinking glass
- ❑ Can of soft drink
- ❑ Match

procedure ☆

1. Fill the glass about half full of soft drink.
2. While the drink is still fizzing, light the match and lower the flame into the top part of the glass. Be careful not to burn yourself.

Carbon dioxide gas will put out a flame.

results ☆ The flame should go out. In 1768, English chemist Joseph Priestley became interested in gases. Because he lived next door to a brewery, he was able to use carbon dioxide, which was used in the brewing process. Priestley soon discovered that when he dissolved carbon dioxide in water, it turned into a refreshing drink— carbonated water. Carbon dioxide gives sparkle and a biting taste to many of today's bubbly drinks.

Joseph Priestley (1733–1804) was born near Leeds, Yorkshire, England, on March 13, 1733. He studied to become a minister at Daventry Academy, but his religious views often got him into trouble. He found more stable employment as a teacher at Warrington Academy in Lancashire and became better known for his contributions to science. In 1793, Priestley and his wife left England for the United States. He died on February 6, 1804, at Northumberland, Pennsylvania.

further ☆ **studies** If a can of soft drink is vigorously shaken, could it be used as a fire extinguisher? (Don't try this experiment without an adult present.) What is carbon dioxide called when it is in a solid form? Look up *dry ice* in an encyclopedia and find out how dry ice is made.

did you ☆ **know?**
❏ That when dry ice melts, there is no liquid. It simply turns back into a gas.
❏ That since carbon dioxide is about one and a half times heavier than air, it can be poured from one container to another.

17
Who first discovered that oxygen is necessary for fire?

materials ☆   ❏ Small candle
      ❏ Matches
      ❏ Metal lid from pop bottle
      ❏ Jar

procedure ☆   1. Ask an adult for permission to light the candle. When the candle is burning, let a few drops of melted wax drip into the lid. Be careful not to burn yourself. Stand the candle in the wax. The wax will harden quickly, holding the candle upright.

Make a base for the candle.

2. Turn the jar upside down and place it over the burning candle.

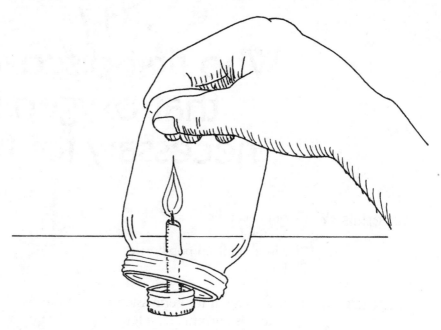

Place the jar over the candle.

results ☆ The flame will burn for a while and then go out. The flame needs oxygen to burn. When the jar was placed over the candle, the flame began to consume the oxygen inside the jar. Soon there wasn't enough oxygen left to support the flame.

In 1771, English chemist Joseph Priestley conducted experiments that showed that when a burning candle converted a chamber of air into carbon dioxide, the air could be restored by a plant. In 1772, French chemist Antoine-Laurent Lavoisier's experiments made him believe that burning or rusting came about through a combination of the burning object and something in the air. In 1774, Lavoisier concluded that air was made up of two gases, oxygen and nitrogen, and that it was oxygen that supported burning or rusting and animal life. He further understood, from studying Priestley's work, that plants consume carbon dioxide and produce oxygen.

Antoine Laurent Lavoisier (1743–1794) was born into a wealthy family on August 26, 1743, in Paris, and was educated by the best scholars. By 1783, he had solved the connection between oxygen and fire, and through further experiments, he discovered the process of oxidation. He became one of the most honored men in science. In 1791, Lavoisier was appointed to a position in the treasury, but he was later accused of cheating the government by French revolutionaries. He was executed in Paris on May 8, 1794.

further ☆ studies Place a small wad of moist steel wool in a jar and turn the jar upside down. Set it aside for a couple of days until the steel wool is well rusted. Then lift the jar and trap the air inside with your hand. Have an adult light a match and quickly stick it inside the jar. The flame should go out. Does rust consume oxygen? Is rust a form of very slow burning?

did you ☆ know?
❐ That the first gunpowder was used by the Chinese for fireworks before guns were invented, and by about 1,000 A.D., they were using it to make small bombs.
❐ That oxygen is the most plentiful of the elements on earth.
❐ That oxygen makes up about 65 percent of our bodies.

18
Who first proposed the atomic theory?

materials ☆
- ❏ Clear drinking glass
- ❏ Magnifying glass
- ❏ Water
- ❏ Sheet of paper
- ❏ Straight pin

procedure ☆

1. Turn the glass upside down and place a drop of water on the bottom of the glass. Examine the water under a magnifying glass.
2. Examine the thickness of a sheet of paper under the magnifying glass.
3. Hold the straight pin in one hand and look closely at the head of the pin.

results ☆ You would be unable to see any atoms, but the drop of water contained more than 33 billion billion molecules. Each one of these molecules is made up of three atoms, two hydrogen and one oxygen. Your drop of water contains more than 100 billion billion atoms. The hydrogen atom is the smallest atom. One million hydrogen atoms stacked on end would not be as tall as the thickness of the sheet of paper. If one atom was as large as the head of the pin, the atoms in one grain of sand would make a block 1 mile square. Everything is made up of atoms. The atom is like a tiny solar system with the nucleus in the center, like the sun. The rest of the atom is mostly empty space that contains even smaller negative electrical charges called *electrons*.

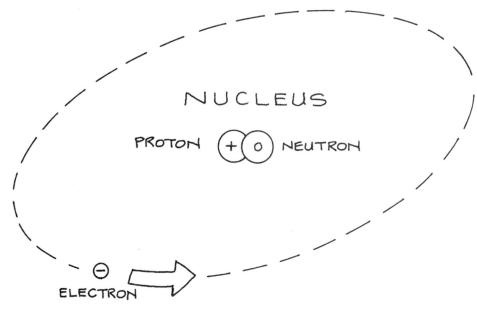

Think of an atom as a tiny solar system.

About 400 B.C., the Greek philosopher Democritus proposed that if matter were divided into smaller and smaller pieces, it eventually could no longer be divided. The name given for this smallest bit of matter was *atom*, Greek for "not cuttable."

In 1803, English chemist John Dalton proposed that all elements are made up of atoms that could not be created, destroyed, or divided. He also believed that atoms of the same element were alike, and were different from the atoms of any other element. Dalton concluded that atoms of unlike elements combine in certain ratios to form molecules. Atomic theory continues to develop today as scientist continue to study the atom.

further ☆ studies Although you can't see the molecules in the water, you can discover that there are spaces between them. Fill a cup to the top with warm water. Gently add the last drop so that it doesn't overflow, then carefully see how many teaspoons of sugar you can add to the water without spilling. The sugar will fit in the spaces between the molecules.

John Dalton (1766–1844), an English chemist and pioneer of modern atomic theory, was born on September 6, 1766, and earned his living by teaching and lecturing until 1833. Dalton studied the atmosphere and experimented with gases, which led to the development of his atomic theory. He proposed his atomic theory of matter in 1803. Dalton died on July 27, 1844.

Check with your local museum to see if they have any exhibits showing how atoms make up molecules that make up everything around us.

Look up *atom, particle accelerator,* and *superconducting cyclotron* in an encyclopedia. What is the nucleus, proton, and neutron of an atom? What happens when scientists smash speeding antiprotons into counter rotating beams of protons?

did you ☆ know?

❏ That the lightest and simplest atom is the hydrogen atom. The nucleus is made up of just one proton and only one electron is in orbit around the nucleus.

❏ That the heaviest and most complicated atom is uranium. It has 92 electrons spinning in seven orbits around the nucleus.

19
Who discovered penicillin?

materials ☆ ❏ Small piece of bread
　　　　　　　 ❏ Water
　　　　　　　 ❏ Jar
　　　　　　　 ❏ Magnifying glass

procedure ☆ 1. Expose the bread to the air in the room for a few hours.
　　　　　　　 2. Wet the bread with water.
　　　　　　　 3. Place the bread in the jar. Put the jar in a dark place for a few
　　　　　　　　　 days then examine the bread with a magnifying glass.

Mold is a plant that cannot manufacture its own food.

results ☆ You should see a fuzzy white growth on the bread, called *mold*. Mold is a tiny, simple plant which belongs to the fungi group. Molds cannot manufacture their own food so they must live on food made by other plants or animals. There are several kinds of molds. In London in 1928, Scottish scientist Alexander Fleming was about to discard a culture of germs he had left uncovered for a few days when he noticed a mold growing on the culture. Under closer examination, he found that the germs next to the mold were dissolving. He experimented with the mold and found that it was closely related to ordinary bread mold. He then grew the mold on a clear, thin soup and found that the soup stopped the growth of bacteria. He called the soup *penicillin*. Later the word *penicillin* was given to only the active chemical substance that formed on the soup.

Sir Alexander Fleming (1881–1955) was a Scottish bacteriologist, born on a farm in Darvel, Scotland. He received his medical degree in 1906 from St. Mary's Hospital in London. He was at the University of London in 1929 when he reported the germ-killing power of the green mold penicillin notatum, *which led to the production of the antibiotic penicillin. Fleming became director of the Wright-Fleming Institute of St. Mary's Hospital in 1947. He died on March 11, 1955.*

further studies ☆ Where else can you find molds? Is mildew a mold? Most moldy foods should be thrown away, but are there any useful molds? What effect does mold have on some cheeses such as Roquefort? Since penicillin kills germs, is it a germicide? Doctors usually give penicillin in the form of an injection in a muscle. A few people are allergic to penicillin. Even small amounts can cause discomfort. Are you allergic to penicillin?

did you ☆ know?

☐ That penicillin is an antibiotic, and that an antibiotic is something that destroys, or stops the growth of, bacteria.

☐ That penicillin was developed in large quantities in the United States during World War II, and reserved almost entirely for military use. It was, however, easily available to the public in the late 1940s.

20
Who discovered/produced the first aluminum?

materials ☆
- ☐ Watch or timer
- ☐ Magnetic compass
- ☐ Aluminum pot
- ☐ Iron pot (both pots should be about the same size)
- ☐ Stove
- ☐ Water

procedure ☆

1. Watch the needle and slowly lower the compass inside the aluminum pot. Now remove the compass. Notice any deflection of the needle.

Watch the compass needle for any change.

2. Repeat step 1 using the iron pot. Notice any movement of the needle.
3. Pour equal amounts of water in each pot.
4. Ask an adult for permission to use the stove. Place the aluminum pot of water on the stove and time how long it takes the water to come to a boil. Then remove the pot. Be sure to use a hot pad or oven mitt to protect your hands.
5. Repeat step 4 with the iron pot of water.

results ☆ When you lowered the compass inside the aluminum pot, the needle continued to point north. But with the iron pot, the needle might point in any direction or could even swing back and forth. Aluminum is not magnetic; iron is magnetic. You also found that the aluminum pot heated the water faster than the iron pot. Aluminum is a better conductor of heat than iron.

In 1807, British chemist Humphry Davy treated clay with sulfuric acid and found that the clay contained an unknown metal he called *aluminum*. But it formed a compound with the oxygen in the air, which he could not separate. He called the compound *alumina*.

The first aluminum was produced in 1825 by Danish chemist Hans Christian Oersted. He heated aluminum chloride and potassium-mercury until it evaporated, leaving a tiny lump of aluminum. For years aluminum was too expensive to be of practical use. Then in 1886, two men, without any knowledge of each other, developed the same process at the same time. Charles Martin Hall of Thompson, Ohio, and Paul Heroult of Paris, France, used the mineral cryolite to dissolve the alumina of Davy's experiment and make it conduct electricity. The process became known as the "Hall–Heroult" process and provided an inexpensive way to make aluminum. In 1888, Hall formed the Pittsburgh Reduction Company and began producing aluminum. In 1907, the company changed its name to the Aluminum Company of America, or ALCOA.

Hans Christian Oersted (1777–1851) was born on August 14, 1777, and received his doctorate from the University of Copenhagen in 1799. Known mostly for his work in electromagnetism, he also studied gases and liquids and became director of the Polytechnic Institute in Copenhagen in 1829. Oersted died on March 9, 1851.

Charles Martin Hall (1863–1914) was born in Thompson, Ohio, on December 6, 1863. He graduated from Oberlin College, and on February 23, 1886, discovered the process that became the foundation of producing aluminum we know today. In April 1886, Paul-Louis-Toussaint Heroult received a French patent for the same process. Hall applied for a United States patent in 1886 but did not get it until 1889. Later he was sued for using the Heroult process but won the case in 1893. Hall died at Daytona Beach, Florida, on December 27, 1914.

further ☆ Look around your home. How many places can you find aluminum
studies being used? Does your house have aluminum windows? Is
aluminum an important metal to the aircraft industry? Many
houses have aluminum siding that looks just like wood.

did you ☆ ❏ That Hall and Heroult were both 22 years old when they
know? discovered the process for producing aluminum, and that they
both died in 1914.
❏ That before 1859, aluminum cost about $550 per pound.
❏ That by the 1950s, the world production of aluminum was
more than 3 million tons a year.
❏ That aluminum can be recycled for less than 5 percent of the
energy used for making the new metal. In the United States,
more than half of the aluminum used in making new cans is
provided by recycling old ones. Today, almost half of the total
aluminum we use is produced through recycling of aluminum
scrap.

21
Who first
discovered plastic?

materials ☆
- ❑ Milk
- ❑ Small pot
- ❑ Stove
- ❑ Food coloring (your choice for color)
- ❑ Tablespoon
- ❑ Vinegar
- ❑ Tea strainer
- ❑ Paper towels
- ❑ Jar

procedure ☆

1. Pour about 10 ounces (.3 liter) of milk in the pot. Ask an adult for permission to warm the milk on the stove. Do not bring it to a boil. Add a couple of drops of food coloring for color. Then add about a tablespoon of vinegar and stir the solution. Continue stirring as clumps form on the surface of the solution.

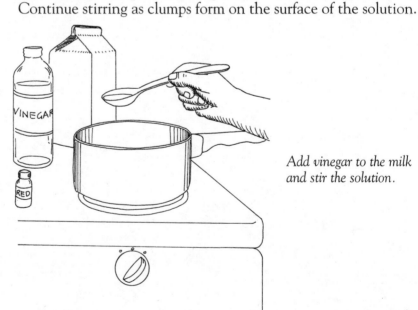

Add vinegar to the milk and stir the solution.

2. Place the tea strainer on the jar and pour the solution through the strainer. Use the spoon to press the clumps and squeeze out most of the liquid.

Use the spoon to press out most of the liquid.

3. Remove the material from the strainer and place it on a paper towel. Use paper towels to remove any excess moisture and work the material as you would a piece of clay. Shape it by hand or press it into a mold. Now set it aside for a few days to dry.

results ☆ The solid that formed on the milk is called *casein*. It separates as curd when milk sours. It also separates from milk when an acid, such as vinegar, is added. In your experiment, you used casein to make a type of plastic. Casein is used in industry to make paints, glue, and some plastic articles. However, there are several different kinds of plastics, and each type is made by a different process using different materials. For example, limestone is added to plastics used for vinyl floor tile, and coal and natural gas are used in the process that makes polystyrene.

In 1855, British chemist Alexander Parkes discovered that when pyroxylin, a type of cellulose, is dissolved in a mixture of alcohol, camphor, and ether, it produces a hard material upon evaporation. This material was the first synthetic plastic, but Parkes could find no commercial use for the product.

In 1869, American printer John Wesley Hyatt and his brother, Isaiah, improved on Parkes's experiments with pyroxylin and produced a material they called *celluloid*. It was the first commercially successful plastic, and was used to make many things, including shirt collars.

further ☆ studies
Make a list of things in your home made of plastic. Remember, there many different types of plastic. Bakelite is the trade name for a type of plastic used to make electrical insulating products. It is named for American chemist Leo H. Baekeland. Is your telephone made from Bakelite?

What happens to plastic containers when they are thrown away? Will plastic rot if it is buried in the earth, or will it last hundreds of years? It has been estimated that one-third of the our nation's landfills have now reached their capacity and room for new landfill is very limited. Large incinerators are replacing landfills, but they produce pollution problems. Today, scientists are working on new ways to recycle plastics and to develop plastics that degrade in landfills. Could recycled plastic be used as a fuel? What ways can you think of to reuse plastics?

Leo Hendrik Baekeland (1863–1944) was the Belgian-American chemist who invented Bakelite in 1909, the first in a series of plastic resins. He spent years in research and received 400 patents for his final product.

did you ☆ know?

❏ That when John Hyatt invented celluloid, he was trying to win a $10,000 prize for a substitute for ivory to make billiard balls.

❏ That shirt collars made of celluloid were highly flammable.

❏ That today, thousands of different plastics exist and new ones are being developed every day.

❏ That plastic foams are recycled into furniture frames and garbage cans, and bottles are shredded into fiber to be reused in several industries. Because different types of plastic are used to make containers, some states require that containers be marked showing the type of plastic used, making recycling easier.

Part 4
The young physicist

Physics is a term that comes from a Greek word that means nature. It is the science that studies the "how" and "why" of the natural world around us. Physics explains why smoke rises, what causes lightning and thunder, and how a satellite stays in orbit.

During the second century B.C., the laws of the lever were discovered along with the principles of the weight of floating bodies. During the Middle Ages, however, few people were interested in physics, and little progress was made for hundreds of years. Fortunately, in the mid-1500s and early 1600s, scientists such as Leonardo da Vinci, Galileo Galilei, William Harvey, and Isaac Newton came along and rekindled the study of physics.

By the late 1800s, Marie and Pierre Curie became famous for their discovery, in 1898, of the element radium. Pierre Curie's earlier work included the study of crystals and their ability to produce small amounts of electricity

Pierre Curie, the French physicist, in 1882 headed the laboratory at the Ecole de Physique et de Chime Industrielle in Paris. He obtained his doctorate in 1894 and married Maria Sklodowska (Marie Curie) that same year.

Marie Curie was born Maria Sklodowska in Warsaw, Poland, and suffered many years as an underpaid teacher and governess before going to Paris to study mathematics and physics. In the spring of 1894, she met Pierre Curie. For her doctoral thesis, Marie began studying radiation, which had recently been discovered. Pierre joined in his wife's work and today they are best known for their pioneering work in the study of radioactivity.

(*piezoelectricity*). He also discovered that the magnetic properties of iron and nickel disappear when they are heated to a certain temperature, then reappear when they are cooled. This temperature varies with different materials and is known as the Curie point.

Marie Curie studied physics and mathematics in Paris and by 1894 held degrees in both subjects. During World War I, she studied the use of X rays in the radioactive materials and their medical applications. Marie Curie died of leukemia on July 4, 1934, as a result of her prolonged exposure to radiation.

During the 1950s, the United States and the Soviet Union both conducted extensive research on nuclear weapons and independently launched the first artificial satellites. On July 20, 1969, Neil Armstrong stepped from his spacecraft onto the moon and said, "That's one small step for man, one giant leap for mankind." Because of these recent advances, branches of physics now include biophysics, solid-state physics, and astrophysics.

22
Who discovered the principles of specific gravity?

materials ☆ ❏ String
 ❏ Rock
 ❏ Spring scales
 ❏ Pencil and note pad
 ❏ Bucket of water

procedure ☆ **1.** Fasten the string to the rock and then attach it to the scales. Weigh the rock in free air and record the weight on the pad.

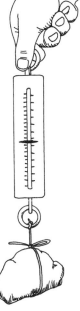

Weigh the rock in free air.

2. Completely submerge the rock in the water and record the new weight. Compare the weights.

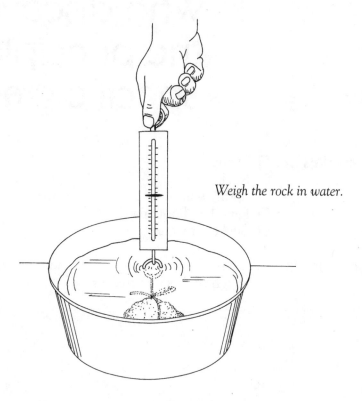

Weigh the rock in water.

results ☆ The specific gravity is the weight of the rock in free air divided by the amount of weight it lost in the water. For example, if the rock weighs 5 pounds in the air and 3 pounds when submerged in water, subtract 3 from 5, which means the rock displaced 2 pounds of water. Divide the weight in air by the weight of the water it displaced, 5 divided by 2, to find the specific gravity of the rock: 2.5.

About 260 B.C., Hiero, the king of Syracuse, Sicily, thought his metalworkers had stolen some of his gold. To hide their crime, they had alloyed the gold with silver. Hiero commanded the Greek mathematician and inventor Archimedes to find out if the royal crown was made of pure gold. Legend has it that while in his bath, Archimedes noticed that his body displaced a volume of water equal to that of his body. He knew that a crown made of gold and some lighter metal would be bulkier than one of pure gold. It would displace more water than an equal amount of pure gold. He immersed equal weights of both in water and noted how far the water level rose in each case. He found that the king's crown was indeed not made of pure gold. You can read more about Archimedes in experiment 4 in part 1 of this book.

further studies ☆ Place the bucket in a pan to catch the overflow of water. Fill the bucket to the top and then submerge the rock in the water. Weigh the water that overflowed into the pan and compare it to the weight of the rock in free air. Float an empty bowl on top of the water, fill the bucket to the top, and then place a rock in the bowl. Weigh the water that spilled over the top and compare it to the weight of the rock in the bowl. Are both weights the same? Must the water displaced by a ship equal the weight of the ship plus the cargo?

did you know? ☆
- ❏ That Archimedes invented a huge rock-throwing catapult that prevented the Romans from conquering Syracuse for three years.
- ❏ That he designed large mirrors that worked like solar furnaces that set fire to the sails of invading ships.
- ❏ That when the Romans finally managed to invade Syracuse, the Roman commander, Marcellus, ordered his soldiers not to harm Archimedes. But it is said that a soldier found him drawing geometric designs in the sand and killed him. As a mathematician and physicist, Archimedes was a genius.

23
Who discovered the laws of gases or fluids in motion?

materials ☆
- ☐ Scissors
- ☐ Thread
- ☐ Two Ping-Pong balls
- ☐ Drinking straw
- ☐ Cellophane tape

procedure ☆ 1. Cut two pieces of thread about 12 inches (30.48 cm) long. Tape one piece to each Ping-Pong ball.

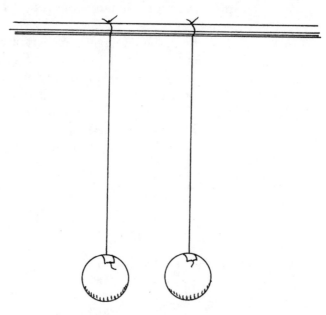

Suspend the balls from a support.

2. Suspend the balls from a support so that they are at the same level and about 1 inch (2.54 cm) apart.

3. Use the straw to send a stream of air between the two balls.

results ☆ When you blow through the straw, the balls quickly move together. The reason they move is because when air moves, its pressure drops. The faster it moves, the lower its pressure. When the stream of air passed between the balls, the air pressure between the balls dropped. Normal air pressure on the other sides of the balls forced the balls closer together. This principle is known as the Bernoulli effect, or Bernoulli's Law.

Daniel Bernoulli was a Swiss mathematician who, in 1738, discovered that the pressure of air is lowered as the speed of the air is increased. This principle allows an airplane to fly and a baseball pitcher to throw a curve ball.

Daniel Bernoulli (1700–1782) was born on February 8, 1700. He began his studies in philosophy and logic but later turned to mathematics and mechanics. He is best known for his work in fluid mechanics and Bernoulli's Law, published in 1738. Bernoulli is considered one of the pioneers of the kinetic theory of gases. He died on March 17, 1782.

further ☆ Hold a sheet of paper in front of your mouth and blow across the
studies top. Does the paper try to rise? Notice a flag waving in the breeze.
Does it curve in ripples? Does this mean that the air pressure on
each side of the flag is changing? What is the difference between
the top of an airplane wing and the bottom? Would moving water
act the same way as air?

did you ☆ ❒ That Bernoulli was the family name of three Swiss mathemati-
know? cians—two brothers, Jacob and John, and Daniel, who was
John's son.
❒ That the curved top of a motorcycle helmet creates lift at high
speeds?

24
Who discovered the laws of the flow of electricity?

materials ☆
- ❏ Thin copper wire
- ❏ Flashlight bulb
- ❏ Flashlight battery
- ❏ Cellophane tape
- ❏ Full length of pencil lead from a mechanical pencil

procedure ☆

1. Ask an adult to help you. Twist one end of the wire tightly around the metal base of the bulb. Connect the other end of the wire to the top of the battery and fasten it in place with tape.
2. Place the pencil lead on a flat surface and rest the bottom of the battery on one end of the piece of lead.
3. Touch the bottom of the bulb to the lead close to the battery. Notice the brightness of the bulb.
4. Slowly slide the bulb down the length of the lead. Notice how the brightness of the bulb changes.

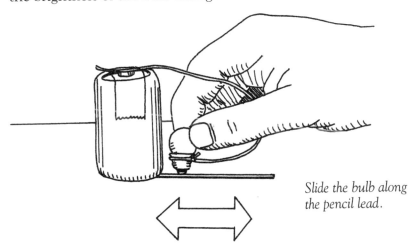

Slide the bulb along the pencil lead.

results ☆ The bulb slowly glows dimmer. The experiment demonstrates that the flow of an electrical current depends on the length of the conductor (pencil lead in this case) and the type of material of the conductor. The pencil lead is not a good conductor, but if copper wire had been used, you would have required a few hundred feet of wire for the demonstration.

In 1827, German physicist Georg Simon Ohm worked out the system of the flow of an electrical current. By using wires of different lengths and thicknesses, he found that the flow of electricity depended on the size of the wire as well as its length. The larger the wire, the more current it could carry; however, over distance, the current was reduced. He had discovered the mathematical resistance of an electrical circuit that is known today as Ohm's Law. Ohm's Law deals with the relationship between the voltage, resistance, and current in an electrical circuit. Basically, the relationship can be written as $V = I \times R$, where V is the voltage producing the current, I is the current in the circuit, and R is the resistance of the circuit to the current. If you substitute simple numbers for the formula, you see that if the voltage stays the same, but the resistance is doubled, the current is reduced by half.

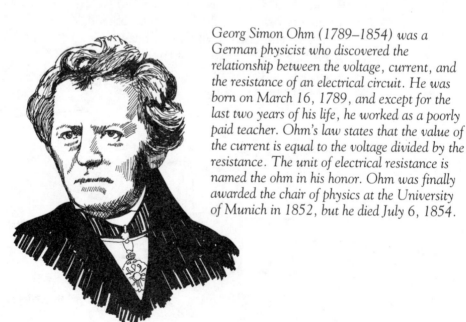

Georg Simon Ohm (1789–1854) was a German physicist who discovered the relationship between the voltage, current, and the resistance of an electrical circuit. He was born on March 16, 1789, and except for the last two years of his life, he worked as a poorly paid teacher. Ohm's law states that the value of the current is equal to the voltage divided by the resistance. The unit of electrical resistance is named the ohm in his honor. Ohm was finally awarded the chair of physics at the University of Munich in 1852, but he died July 6, 1854.

further ☆ Substitute a copper wire in the experiment. Can you see any
studies   difference in the brightness? Is copper a better conductor than
graphite? Could graphite be used to control the current? With the
help of an adult, straighten a wire coat hanger and try it in place
of the lead. Is it a good conductor?

did you ☆ ❏ That the resistance of a conductor, or a device placed in the
know?   circuit, is measured in units called *ohms*.
            ❏ That Ohm's work was largely neglected in Germany until the
              British scientists of the Royal Society of London awarded him
              its Copley Medal in 1841.

25

Who invented the miner's safety lamp?

materials ☆ ❒ Wire screen (old tea strainer)
❒ Candle and matches
❒ Piece of paper

procedure ☆ 1. Ask an adult for permission to light the candle. Turn the tea strainer upside down and hold the screen over the flame of the candle. The screen should be just above the tip of the flame.
2. Lower the piece of paper until it is almost touching the screen.

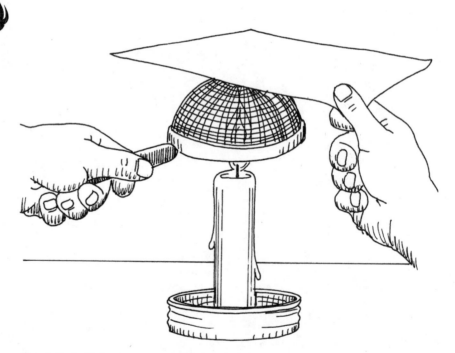

Carefully hold the paper over the screen.

3. Don't forget to blow out the candle when you are done with the experiment.

results ☆ You will notice that the flame did not come through the screen and that the paper did not burn. The reason is because the heat of the flame is conducted away by the wires in the screen, and the screen keeps the paper from reaching the temperature necessary for ignition.

In 1815, English scientist Sir Humphry Davy was commissioned to study mine explosions. His research led him to invent the miner's safety lamp. The Davy lamp was an oil lamp whose flame was contained inside metal gauze. Light and air could pass through the gauze, but it prevented the heat from the flame from causing an explosion.

Sir Humphry Davy (1778–1829) was an English chemist and physicist who invented the miner's safety lamp in 1851. His lamp greatly reduced the risks of coal-mine explosions. Davy was born December 17, 1778. He studied medicine but turned to chemistry in 1797. Davy was a popular lecturer at the Royal Institute in London, where he became a professor in 1802. He was knighted in 1812 and made a baronet in 1818. Davy died on May 29, 1829.

further ☆
studies

Wrap a coin tightly in an old handkerchief. Hold the coin over a candle flame. Does the metal coin keep the cloth from burning? Why does the gas engine of a lawn mower have fins around the spark plug? Is metal a good conductor of heat?

did you ☆
know?

❑ That at the age of 20, Davy experimented with nitrous oxide (laughing gas) and encouraged its use as one of the first anesthetics.

❑ That in 1808, Davy invented the electric arc that is used in welding today.

❑ That when women scientists were few, and rarely received any credit for their work, Hertha Marks Ayrton conducted acclaimed research in the study of the electric arc and was made a member of the Institute of Electrical Engineers in 1899. She also invented an antigas fan for the British War Office. More than 100,000 were used during World War I.

❑ That in 1813, before he became famous, Michael Faraday worked for Davy as a laboratory bottle washer.

26
Who is the ancestor of today's photography?

materials ☆
- ❑ Round oatmeal box
- ❑ Utility knife
- ❑ Dull black paint
- ❑ Old newspapers
- ❑ Piece of aluminum foil about 2 inches (5.08 cm) square
- ❑ Needle
- ❑ Masking tape
- ❑ Roll of 120 black and white film (slow speed)
- ❑ Scissors
- ❑ Watch with second hand

procedure ☆

1. Make sure all dust particles have been removed from the box. Ask an adult to help you. Carefully cut a 1-inch- (2.54-cm-) square opening in the center of the side of the box. Always cut away from yourself.
2. Spray or brush the lid and inside of the box with dull black paint. Allow the paint to dry.
3. Smooth the aluminum foil to remove any wrinkles and make a tiny hole in the center with the point of the needle.
4. Place the aluminum foil on the outside of the box with the pinhole in the center of the 1-inch (2.54-cm) opening. Fasten it in place with masking tape. Tape all the edges so that no light can leak in. You now have a pinhole camera.
5. To load the film, take the roll of film, the pinhole camera, scissors, and masking tape to a bathroom or closet where no light can come in. Place the items on a counter where you can find them in the dark. With the light off, pull about 8 inches (20.32 cm) of film from the roll. Cut the film about 1 inch (2.54 cm) from the roll. Cut about 3 inches from the other end (the end with the tab). You should have a curved strip about 4 inches (10.16 cm) long.

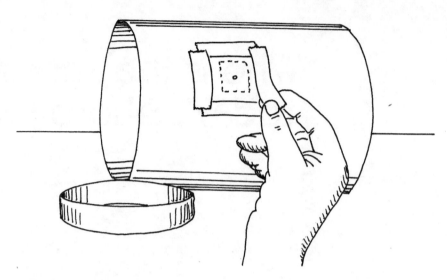

Tape the edges completely to keep out the light.

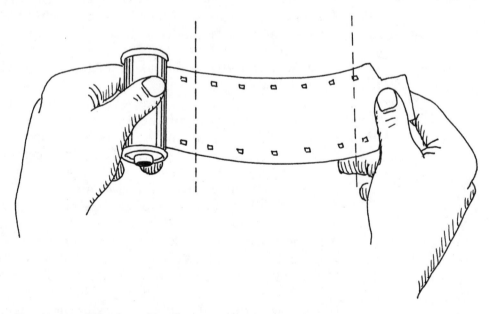

Cut a piece of film from the roll.

6. Place the curved strip inside the box on the side opposite the pinhole. Fit the curve of the film with the curve of the box. Fasten the ends of the film to the box with masking tape. Place the lid on the box and tape it in place to keep out unwanted light. Hold your hand over the pinhole and take your camera outside into bright sunlight.

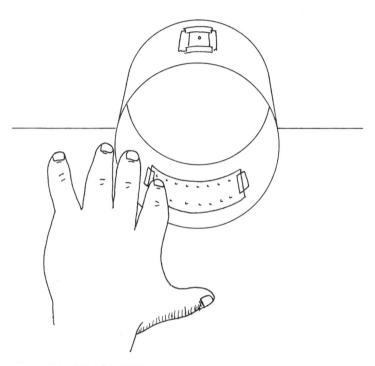

Fasten the film opposite the pinhole.

7. Pick out a subject and place the camera on a solid surface. Aim the hole at the subject and remove your hand for about 60 seconds. Cover the hole with your hand and return to the dark room. Remove the film and place it in the plastic, light-tight container that came with the roll of film. Have the film developed and a print made.

Light rays travel from the subject through the pinhole and strike the film attached to the other side of the box. The film is sensitive to light and reacts to the image in front of the pinhole. When the film is developed, a negative image is produced. The negative is then used to print the picture.

Around 1835, French inventor and painter Louis J. Daguerre discovered one of the first forms of photographic print. He first described the process in 1839. It was called *daguerreotype* after its inventor.

Louis J. Daguerre (1787–1851) was a French inventor and pioneer of photography. He was born on November 18, 1787. He trained as a painter but was popular for his elaborate stage productions. In 1839, he developed a process for making photographic prints on silver-coated copper plates. Daguerre died on July 10, 1851.

At about the same time, British scientist William H. Fox Talbot invented a photographic technique that used sensitized paper to produce both negatives and prints. Talbot's process is the ancestor of the one we use today.

In 1879, American George Eastman invented a machine for coating glass plates used for photography. In 1883, he perfected flexible roll films, and by 1888, Eastman had produced a light camera suitable for the general public. He called it the Kodak.

William Henry Talbot (1800–1877) was the British scientist known for inventing the negative-process of photography. He was born February 11, 1800, and first fixed a photographic image on sensitive paper in 1835. By 1841, Talbot had perfected his process that produced negatives from which any number of positive copies could be made. He died on September 17, 1877.

George Eastman (1854–1932) was born on July 12, 1854, at Waterville, New York. He started the Eastman Kodak Company in 1880 and introduced flexible film in 1884. Eastman produced the Kodak box camera in 1888 and sold more than 100,000 cameras to amateur photographers within two years. He contributed large sums to schools and colleges, and his company was the first in the United States to provide the employees with a profit-sharing plan. Eastman died on March 14, 1932.

Who is the ancestor of today's photography?

further ☆
studies

How many ways can you think of in which photography is used today? Could a camera capture high-speed images we otherwise couldn't see? Could time exposures be used to study plant growth?

did you ☆
know?

❏ That Eastman's Kodak of 1888 was priced at $25, but by 1900 he had a camera on the market for $1.

❏ That Talbot published the first book that was illustrated with photographs. It's title was *The Pencil of Nature*.

27
Who invented the gyroscope?

materials ☆
- ❏ Length of string about 4 feet (1.2 m) long
- ❏ Toothpick or paper clip
- ❏ Phonograph record or similar flat disk

procedure ☆

1. Tie one end of the string around the middle of the toothpick and thread it through the hole in the record.
2. Hold the other end of the string and suspend the record a few inches above the floor. Start the record to swing slowly from side to side like a pendulum. Notice how the record tilts as it swings.

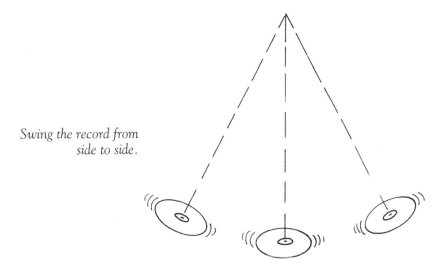

Swing the record from side to side.

3. Hold the record level and give it a spin. Now swing it a few inches from the floor.

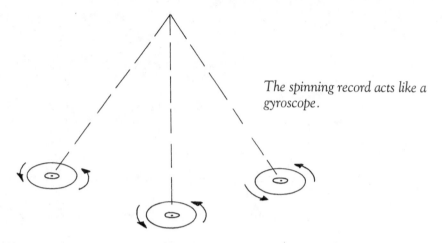

The spinning record acts like a gyroscope.

results ☆ When the record was spinning, it seemed to float level above the floor. It continues to float level until it almost stops spinning. As long as the record is spinning, it remains in the same plane, or attitude, it had when it started to spin. The record has become a gyroscope.

In 1851, French physicist Leon Foucault suspended a 62-pound iron ball about 2 feet (60.96 cm) in diameter from a steel wire over 200 feet (60.96 m) long, from inside the dome of a church in Paris. The bottom of the ball came to a point just above the floor. The ball was pulled far to one side and the pendulum was started to swing. The swinging pendulum would remain in the same plane except for the rotation of the earth. Spectators were able to watch the pendulum change its angle of swing relative to the earth as the earth turned. In 1852, Foucault demonstrated a device with a rapidly spinning wheel that resisted any change in its axis—the *gyroscope*. Around 1900, more ships were being built of steel instead of wood, making magnetic compasses unreliable. Because a gyroscope maintains the same angle in relation to the stars, it became a better substitute.

further ☆ Any spinning object has a tendency to resist a change of direction
studies in its axis. Hold a bicycle wheel firmly by its axle and have a friend give it a spin. Carefully try to tilt the wheel and you can feel this resistance. Does this principle help you ride a bicycle? Would a bicycle stay upright if the wheels were not turning?

Jean Foucault (1819–1868) was the French physicist who demonstrated the rotation of the earth on its axis with a pendulum experiment and also with a gyroscope. He was born September 19, 1819, and in 1845 was the first to photograph the sun. Foucault also is credited with improving telescope mirrors and lenses. He died on February 11, 1868.

did you ☆ know?

❏ That the first gyrocompass was installed in a German warship in 1910.

❏ That in 1911, American scientist and inventor Elmer A. Sperry demonstrated a successful gyrocompass on a U.S. warship.

Elmer Ambrose Sperry (1860–1930) was an American engineer and inventor. He was born on October 21, 1860, and held over 350 patents from a wide range of fields, including aviation, automotive, mining, and gyrocompasses. Sperry became interested in gyroscopes in 1907 and developed a gyrocompass for ships. In 1910, he started the Sperry Gyroscope Company, which later become the Sperry Rand Corporation. He died on June 16, 1930.

Who invented the gyroscope?

28
Who discovered that heat is a form of energy?

materials ☆
- ❒ Length of rigid copper tubing, about 5 feet (1.5 m) long
- ❒ Clamp
- ❒ Table
- ❒ Knitting needle or large nail
- ❒ Cardboard pointer, about 12 inches (30.48 cm) long
- ❒ Hair dryer
- ❒ Glue

procedure ☆

1. Have an adult help you with this experiment. Place the copper tube lengthwise near the edge of the table. Clamp one end to the table and place the knitting needle under the other end. The end of the needle should extend past the edge of the table. Glue the middle of the cardboard pointer to the end of the needle.

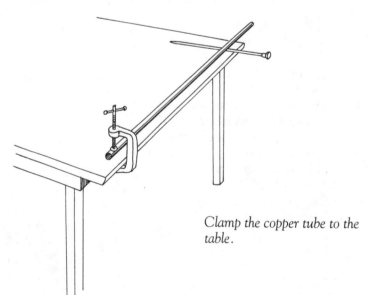

Clamp the copper tube to the table.

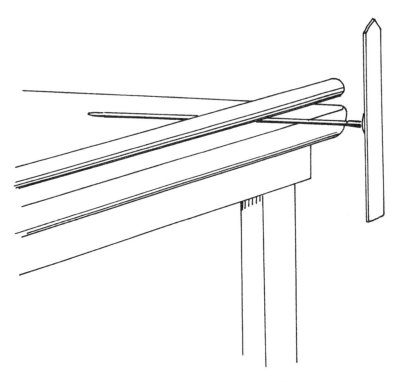

The expanding tube should cause the knitting needle to move.

2. Turn the hair dryer on high heat and blow hot air through the tube from the clamped end. Keep your hands on the handle so you don't get burned when the dryer gets hot. Aim the hair dryer so that it doesn't blow directly on the pointer. Does the pointer move?

results ☆ The hot air causes the copper to expand slightly, turning the needle, which moves the pointer.

In 1824, French physicist Nicolas Carnot published his book about the motive power of heat. He was the first scientist to consider the relationship between heat and the efficiency of heat to do work. Carnot is considered the founder of the science of thermodynamics. However, British physicist James Prescott Joule proved that heat was a form of energy; he was the first scientist to measure accurately the relationship between heat energy and mechanical energy. Around 1840, Joule built a machine which used falling weights to turn a paddle wheel in a drum of water. The paddles warmed the water. When he measured the increase in temperature, he found it was precisely related to the distance the weights had fallen.

Nicolas Carnot (1796–1832) was a French physicist and a pioneer of thermodynamics. He was born into a prominent French family on June 1, 1796, and is best known for his studies of heat as a form of energy. Carnot died on August 24, 1832.

James Prescott Joule (1818–1889) was the British physicist known for his work in thermodynamics. He was born on December 24, 1818, and in 1840 published his studies on the heat produced by an electrical current. In 1852, he and William Thomson found that when a gas expands freely, its temperature drops. This principle led to the development of refrigeration. Joule died on October 11, 1889.

further studies ☆ Where can you find energy being used around your home? Is heat also produced? If you briskly rub your hands together, are you changing mechanical energy into heat? Does a toaster change electrical energy into heat energy?

did you know? ☆

❐ That almost 90 percent of the electrical energy used to light a regular light bulb is lost as heat.

❐ That the colder of two bodies will always absorb heat until both are at the same temperature.

❐ That heat waves are transmitted from a body as long as the molecules in the body continue to vibrate, and they will vibrate as long as the temperature of the body is above absolute zero (−459.4°F, −273°C). A temperature of −458°F has been reached.

29
Who discovered the quantum theory of energy?

materials ☆
- ❑ Three pieces of thin cardboard, about 4 × 5 inches (10.16 × 12.7 cm)
- ❑ Flashlight
- ❑ Stack of books
- ❑ Three supports for cardboard
- ❑ Books
- ❑ Small nail
- ❑ Two lenses from discarded polarized sunglasses

procedure ☆

1. Stack and align the three pieces of cardboard. Ask an adult to use the nail to punch a small hole through the cardboard. Stand the cardboard upright about 12 inches (30.48 cm) apart and support them between a couple of books.

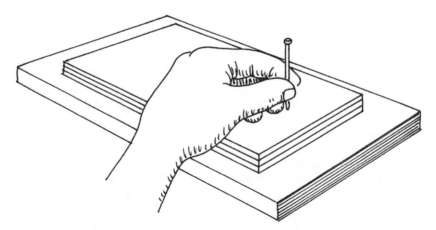

Carefully make a small hole in the cards.

2. Place the flashlight about 12 inches (30.48 cm) from the first card on a stack of books so that it is in line with the holes in the cards. All the holes must be in a straight line with the flashlight. Turn on the flashlight and sight through the holes. Can you see the light? Move one of the cards slightly. Can you still see the light?

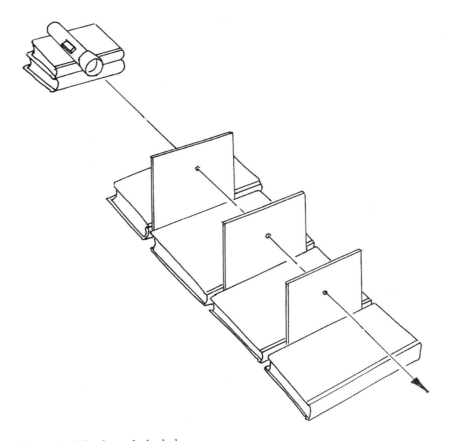

Shine the light through the holes.

3. Place one polarized lens over the other. Hold both lenses level and look at the light. Can you see most of the light?
4. Hold one lens and slowly rotate the other until it is straight up and down. Can you still see any light?

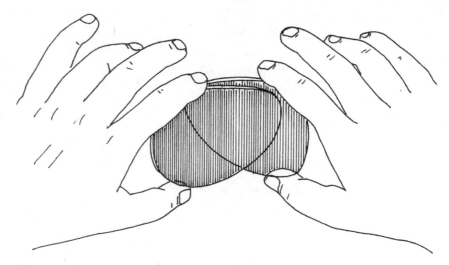

Place one lens over the other.

Rotate one of the lens.

results ☆ Once all of the holes were aligned, you could see the light, but if one of the pieces of cardboard was moved, you could not. Light travels in a straight line.

The lenses of polarized sunglasses are made up of vertical lines. These lines form a grating that acts like a filter to reduce glare from light waves reflecting from shiny surfaces. When one lens is placed over the other, the lens in front polarizes the light coming through it. If the lines in the second lens are lined up with the lines in the front lens, the light can pass through. But when the second lens was rotated, the first lens produced a polarized beam that was unable to pass through the second lens. Most of the light was shut off.

In 1666, English physicist Isaac Newton sent a beam of white light through a prism. The beam separated into various colors, proving that white light is really made up of lights of different colors. Newton further concluded that light was made up of tiny particles he called corpuscles, and that light traveled in a straight line.

Sir Isaac Newton (1643–1727) made important discoveries in astronomy, mathematics, and physics. He was born on January 4, 1643, and began studying at Trinity College at Cambridge University in June 1661. Newton left the university when it was closed by the plague in 1665. He made significant advances in optics during the years of the plague. In 1687, Newton published his book Principia, *in which he described the laws of motion and universal gravitation. The publication made him the leading scientist of the time. He left scientific research in 1693 for a position with the government and was knighted by Queen Ann in 1708. Newton died on March 31, 1727.*

About the same time, Dutch physicist Christian Huygens argued that light traveled in waves. In 1860, English physicist James Clerk Maxwell developed the theory that light was electromagnetic.

Christian Huygens (1629–1695) was the Dutch scientist known for discovering the rings of Saturn (1656), inventing the pendulum clock (1656), and proposing the wave theory of light. He was born on April 14, 1629, and studied at the University of Leiden and the College of Orange. Huygens published his wave theory of light in 1678, but Newton's theory prevailed for many years. He died on July 8, 1695.

James Clerk Maxwell (1831–1879) was the English physicist who made major contributions in the field of electromagnetism and the kinetic theory of gases. He was born on November 13, 1831 and received a degree in mathematics from Trinity College, Cambridge in 1854. Between 1864 and 1873, Maxwell conducted research in the relationship between electricity and magnetism and concluded from his studies that light is an electromagnetic phenomenon. He died on November 5, 1879.

Max Planck (1858–1947) was the German physicist who developed the quantum theory of energy. He was born on April 23, 1858 and received his Ph.D. in 1879 from the University of Munich. Planck began studying blackbody radiation in 1897, which led to his discovery in 1900 of the basic unit of energy, the quantum. He died on October 3, 1947.

In 1900, German physicist Max Planck established the idea that light is made up of little packages of energy called *quanta*. This discovery led to the development of the quantum theory of energy. Planck was the first to realize that the energy of all electromagnetic waves, including light, heat, and radio waves, can exist only in tiny packages, or quanta. Light travels in waves, but is corpuscular in nature. Apparently, Newton, Huygens, and Maxwell were all partly right.

further ☆
studies

The next time you put a hot dog in a microwave oven, realize that microwaves are simply radio waves generated at a high frequency. These waves have enough energy to penetrate the food and heat it. Could microwaves be dangerous? X rays are part of the electromagnetic spectrum, which includes radio waves, heat, and visible light waves. Besides medicine, how many ways can you think of that X rays can be used. Can X rays be used to examine metal castings for flaws? Are they used at airports?

❏ That Max Planck received the Nobel Prize in 1918 for his quantum theory of energy.

❏ That Planck became disgruntled when an unknown Swiss clerk wrote a paper on the theory of relativity and greatly supported Planck's theory. The clerk was Albert Einstein. Later they became close friends and even played chamber music together, Planck at the piano and Einstein on the violin.

Index

photographic processes and
light, 101-106, **102**, **103**
polarization of light, 115,
116, 117
quantum theory of
energy/light, 114-120, **114**,
115, **116**
spectrum of light, 117
wave theory of light, 118
light-years, 41-42
Lilienthal, Otto, German
aeronautical engineer, 9, **10**
Lindbergh, Charles, first
transatlantic flight, 13-14,
13, 17
liquids, 64, 66
motion of fluids, Bernoulli
effect, 92-94, **92**

M
"machine" as defined by
engineering, 26
mapping the sky, 53-55, **53**,
54
Mars, 56, 57, 58
Massachusetts Institute of
Technology (MIT), 61-62
Maxwell, James Clerk,
electromagnetic wave
theory, 118, **118**
mechanical engineering, 4-5
Archimedes, Greek
mathematician/inventor,
25-26, **26**
diesel engines, 32-34, **32**, **33**
Diesel, Rudolf, inventor of
diesel engine, 33-34, **33**
first-, second-, and third-class
levers, 25
fulcrum, 24, **24**, 26
Hero, earliest steam engine,
30, **30**
inclined planes, 25, **25**
lever and screw, 24-26, **24**,
25

"machine" as defined by
engineering, 26
Newcomen, Thomas, early
steam engine design, 30
steam engines, 27-31, **27**, **28**,
30
steam turbines, 31
Watt, James, early patented
steam engine, **29**, 30
medicine
anesthetics, 100
antibiotics, 75
nitrous oxide (laughing gas),
100
penicillin, 73-75, **73**
Woods, Granville T.,
mechanical engineer and
inventor, 31
Mercury, 56, 57
microwaves, 119
mildews, 74
miner's safety lamp, 98-100, **98**
Mitchell, Edgar, moon walk
astronaut, 21
Mizar and Alcor, double-star
system, 59, **60**
molds, penicillin, 73-75, **73**
molecules, 71
Moon's size, speed, and surface
features, 52

N
Neptune, 56, 57
neutron of atom, **71**, 72
Newcomen, Thomas, early
steam engine design, 30
Newton, Isaac, vii, 85
spectrum of light experiments,
117
nitrogen, 64
nitrous oxide (laughing gas),
100
Noonan, Fred, copilot to
Amelia Earhart, 15-16
nucleus of atom, 70, **71**, 72

O
Oersted, Hans Christian,
production of usable
aluminum, 77, **78**
Ohm, Georg, discovery of
current flow, 96, **96**, 97
Ohm's law, 96
ohms as unit of resistance, 97
Olympus Mons, Martian
volcano, 58
Orteign, Raymond, proposed
first transatlantic flight
contest, 14
oxygen, 63, 64
fire and oxidation, 67-69, **67**,
68

P
paper airplane (*see* hang gliders)
Parkes, Alexander, first
synthetic plastic, 82
particle accelerators, 72
penicillin, 73-75, **73**
photographic processes and
light, 101-106, **102**, **103**
Daguerre, Louis J.,
daguerreotypes invented,
104, **104**
daguerreotypes, 104
Eastman, George,
photographic film invented,
104, 105, **105**
high-speed nature
photography, 106
Kodak company, 104
Talbot, William H., modern
photographic process, 104,
105, **105**
physics, 85-120
absolute zero, 112
antiprotons, 72
Archimedes, specific gravity
and displacement
experiment, 25-26, **26**, 90-91
astrophysics, 87
atomic theory, 70-72, **71**

About the Author

Robert W. Wood has professional experience in aviation science, experimental agriculture, electricity, electronics, and science research. He is the author of more than a dozen physics and science books, as well as several home maintenance books. His work has been featured in major newspapers and magazines, and he has been a guest on radio talk shows around the United States. Some of his books have been translated into other languages, including Turkish.

Bob enjoys the wonders of nature and is always interested in the advances of science and how it affects our lifestyles. Although he has traveled and worked worldwide, he now lives with his wife and family in Arkansas.